Boscae
6·84

consumption?, 21-22,
27 fn 21,
38. Annales
33. how structural km, Marxism opposed
34. what was, for Marx, motor of historical change?
  1. forces & relations of production in contradiction
                                    (structure)
  2. class structure (human agency?)
  economism / voluntarism.

In the Tracks
of Historical
Materialism

The Wellek Library Lectures at the
University of California, Irvine

Frank Lentricchia
Series Editor

Perry Anderson

In the Tracks
of Historical
Materialism

The University of Chicago Press
Chicago and London

(1943)

The University of Chicago Press, Chicago 60637
The University of Chicago Press, Ltd., London
© 1983 by Perry Anderson
© 1984 by The University of Chicago
All rights reserved. Published 1984
Printed in the United States of America

93 92 91 90 89 88 87 86 85 84   5 4 3 2 1

Library of Congress Cataloging in Publication Data

Anderson, Perry.
    In the tracks of historical materialism.

    Reprint. Originally published: London : Verso, 1983.
    Includes index.
    1. Philosophy, Marxist—Addresses, essays, lectures.
I. Title.
B809.8.A599   1984   335.4   84-110
ISBN 0-226-01788-5

Contents

Foreword

As historian and historical sociologist, editor of the *New Left Review*, historian of modern Marxist theory, and now generative theorist himself—in *Passages from Antiquity to Feudalism* (1974), *Lineages of the Absolutist State* (1974), *Considerations on Western Marxism* (1976), and *Arguments within English Marxism* (1980), to cite the major titles—Perry Anderson has become over the past fifteen years one of a handful of our premier contemporary Marxists. It was in his landmark *Considerations on Western Marxism*, an intellectual history of Marxist theory in Western Europe from about 1920 to 1968—or roughly after the isolation of the Russian revolution—that Anderson produced what is by wide agreement our most penetrating guide to, and interpretation of modern Marxism. His focus in *Considerations* is trained sharply, and rather exclusively, on the work of Lukács, Korsch, Gramsci, Adorno, Marcuse, Benjamin, Sartre, Althusser, Della Volpe, and Colletti. In this new book, *In the Tracks of Historical Materialism*—the bulk of which was delivered as the second annual series of Wellek Library Lectures at Irvine in May of 1982—Anderson disclaims for several good reasons that he has written a sequel to *Considerations*. The period with which he deals is much shorter; his style here is (in the mode of public speaking) slightly more informal; in the new book, unlike the old, he has had to deal with Marxism in its intellectual context—concurrent developments in contemporary philosophy and critical theory. Still, I do not think it either ungracious of me (given the genre of my remarks) or inaccurate (given what Anderson has written) to say that *In the Tracks of His-*

torical Materialism is, in fact, a kind of sequel to *Considerations on Western Marxism*. Those who have read and appreciated the earlier work are going to see it that way. Those who have not will suffer no disadvantage: they will instead read a gripping account of contemporary theory—one of the few works of contemporary theory (maybe there are three or four others) which we will come back to and recommend to our friends and students. And no small reason for the sort of impact which I imagine for this book will be its stylistic achievement: unusually compressed—in brief compass it evokes the range of current theoretical discussion—witty, polemical, and all the time clear and accessible, even to those, I'd guess, outside the field of twentieth-century Marxism.

In the Tracks of Historical Materialism is comprised of three chapters and a postscript. The first chapter, "Prediction and Performance," contains substantial backward glances at the Western Marxism he had chronicled in the earlier book—an elegant rehearsal of his critique of its intellectualist isolation, its sundering of all bonds that might have linked it to popular movements for revolutionary socialism, and the historical reasons for this fatal drifting apart of theory and practice. As Anderson acerbically notes, in the "High Cold War of the 50s" there was "scarcely a Marxist theoretician of weight who was not a holder of a chair in the academy rather than of a post in the class struggle." Despite its brilliant achievements in epistemology and aesthetics, and its undeniably important explorations in the realms of higher cultural activity, Western Marxism not only reversed Marx's own itinerary (from philosophy to politics to economics) but in so singlemindedly reviving an astringent philosophical discourse it took virtually no interest in *strategic discussion* of the road to "realizable socialism." So even though he is very sympathetic to Western Marxism's immensely difficult historical situation, Anderson does not flinch from pointing out its "lateral relationships to bourgeois culture," its "subjacent pessimism," and its wholesale retreat from the goals of classical Marxism. Nor does he flinch from pointing out that several predictions he had made in *Considerations* about the future course of Marxism, in the wake of its exhaustion in the late 60s, though in some general sense confirmed, do not thereby give Marxists any cause for comfort. For the reunification of theory and popular practice—his major prediction—conspicuously failed to materialize. The dearth of strategic thinking in Western Marxism continues to enervate Marxist thought in general: a "poverty of strategy," says Anderson, not a "poverty of theory."

In the remainder of the opening chapter Anderson gives us a quick survey of the essential work done in Marxism since the late 60s, with emphasis on the surprising emergence of Marxist culture in England and the United States, even as Latin Europe, the site of Western Marxism, witnessed its steep decline. The transition to his second chapter is a brief account of the anticommunist fevers, political and cultural, in Latin Europe: the reversal of Colletti, the changes of Sollers and Kristeva from Maoism to mysticism to celebration of the social order in the United States, the emergence of André Glucksmann, ironic protégé of Althusser—all of this more or less within a setting of accommodation in Western Europe to existing polities.

It is in his second and third chapters, however ("Structure and Subject," "Nature and History"), where Anderson speaks most forcefully on his own as a Marxist theorist, for it is here that he sketches first an account of the defeat of Latin Marxism at the hands of an adversary, structuralism and poststructuralism, that took Marxism on in frontal combat: on the very terrain that Marxism had long claimed to explain better than all others—the relationships between structure and subject, system and agency, in human history and society. Having sketched the engagement and then the victory which, in Anderson's words, made "Paris the center of European intellectual reaction," he proceeds in the most original portion of the book to make his intervention by mounting the most stinging logical attack on structuralist and poststructuralist ideas that I have seen. The persuasiveness of Anderson in these pages lies in part in his willingness to confront structuralism at its sources—particularly Saussure and the linguistic model derived from him. It is the universal deployment of the linguistic model, he argues, that is the cause in structuralism of several "abusive analogies": the "exorbitation of language," the "attenuation of truth," the "randomization of history," and, best irony, the "capsizal of structures." In order to properly evaluate these abuses, Anderson appeals not to Marx but to Saussure for testimony that neither kinship nor the economy are commensurable with the institution of language. Having thus established structuralism's genealogical embarrassment, he then produces an analysis of structuralism and poststructuralism, in his own voice, which shows precisely why those philosophical pretenders to the place of Marxism in France and Italy can have little interest in social change and, in Derrida himself, almost no interest in the exploration of social reality or the defense of a particular political point of view. (On this last point, readers of the Yale school of literary criticism will understand an implicit critique of that practice.) The major exception in Western Europe is Habermas, whose philosophy of language and history, with its sources in Frankfurt school Marxism, does not exclude politics as such—despite its many affinities to structuralism. As Anderson puts it: "Unlike any of his opposite numbers in France, Habermas attempted a direct structural analysis of the imminent tendencies of contemporary capitalism, and of the possibility of system-changing crises arising from them." Anderson concludes his third chapter with a quick sketch of the political fate of international communist movements from the Cold War through Khrushchev, Mao, and Eurocommunism—the practical political contexts of the failure of Latin Marxism and the concomitant rise of structuralism.

In his "Postscript" Anderson takes stock of the relationship between Marxism and socialism, and in the process of doing so must confront the "cognitive pretentions" of the former with the renewed moral and utopian energies of the latter. A proponent of class struggle as the primary historical operator of social change, Anderson enters into sympathetic debate with spokespersons for feminism and the antinuclear movement. He carefully notes (with no defensive qualifications) the inadequacies of Marxist tradition on the subject of women and the transcendent claim of antinuclear proponents on us all in the face of extermination. In addition, he makes an eloquent plea for the integration of these radical movements. But in the end Anderson argues for the primacy of historical materialism: profit is both gender and color blind, and capitalists, no less than socialists, have an obvious interest in staying alive. The pointed implication that feminist and antinuclear movements are not radical enough will of course not go unanswered. On the other hand, that is the sort of bold and lively challenge he has written throughout. *In the Tracks of Historical Materialism* should become a focus for controversy as well as education.

Frank Lentricchia

Preface

The text of this short book needs some explanation. When the Programme in Critical Theory at the University of California at Irvine invited me to give three lectures in a series associated with the Wellek Library, I elected to discuss the contemporary situation of just one such theory. As I had already attempted a sketch in the mid seventies of the evolution of Marxism in Western Europe since the First World War, offering some predictions as to its likely future directions, it seemed opportune to review intellectual developments since then and to look at how my earlier conjectures had fared. The result is not exactly a sequel to *Considerations on Western Marxism*. This is partly because the period with which it deals is too short — scarcely a decade, in effect. Such an interval does not permit the kind of settled retrospect that half-a-century of history can afford. Proportions and relations are always liable to foreshortening from such a close distance — with consequent distortions. The form of the analyses presented here also differs from that earlier account. Spoken as lectures, in an academic setting, they employ a more informal address than would the ordinary page, one involving more frequent use of the personal pronoun. It seemed artificial to alter this after the event; but it remains a feature to be excused. Another peculiarity of the text, as will be seen, is its initial set at the subject: introduced under the rubric of general remarks on the notion of 'critical theory' itself, and its ambiguities.

One other departure from the lines of the previous study may be noted. On this occasion, a survey of recent developments within Marxism was not practicable without some consideration of con-current philosophical developments outside it, as they affected, or appeared to affect, its fortunes. For this reason, the second lecture is largely devoted to a discussion of French structuralism and post-structuralism. My debts here are two-fold. The general inspiration for my treatment of this field I owe to Sebastiano Timpanaro, whose combination of critical scholarship and political fortitude are an example to every socialist of my generation. For more local reflections I owe very much to Peter Dews. His forthcoming book on the subject, *A Critique of French Philosophical Modernism*, incomparably wider in scope and finer in grain, is written with an authority and sympathy I do not possess: its appearance will soon render these pages more or less obsolete. They will have served their purpose if they in any way prepare, albeit in a somewhat dissenting register, for his.

To round off the lectures, I have included a postscript that raises a few problems not directly broached in them – issues which concern the relationship between Marxism and socialism, essentially. In all, the book tries to track the movements of historical materialism over the past years, which took more than one direction. The results could of necessity be no more than an interim reading. As such, they are intended simply to provide a rough guide to some of the changes in the intellectual environment as the seventies passed into the eighties. I am pleased that they appear under a series linked to the name of René Wellek, a doyen of comparative literature and master of the history of criticism itself. His easy internationalism of mind, and committed defence of classical standards of rational argument and appraisal, should command the admiration of anyone attached to the values of Marxism – a body of thought far from his own. At all events, they do mine. At the end of *Discriminations*, Wellek offered his readers 'A Map of Contemporary Criticism in Europe'. Something like that, for historical materialism in North America and Western Europe, is attempted here. I would like to thank especially Frank and Melissa Lentricchia, Mark Poster and Jon Wiener for the opportunity to make the attempt; and for the warmth of their hospitality at Irvine.

1
Prediction and Performance

The term 'critical theory', which brings us here tonight, contains its own peculiar, if productive, ambiguities. Theory, in the first instance, of what? Usages oscillate between two main poles: of literature, most familiarly, as the name and collection which we are honouring remind us. But also of society, as a less widespread but more polemical and pointed tradition would have it. In this second version, the two words that make up the formula often acquire capital letters, as the token of their diacritical distance from the first. The other component of the term raises similar questions. What sort of criticism is being theorized? From what ground, and on what principles? A broad range of possible stances are at stake here, as this series itself, in its catholicity, makes plain. In practice, the very variety of positions within literary criticism, with the attendant attritions and collisions between them, has always tended to implicate the literary with the social, as readers of René Wellek's own *History of Criticism* will be aware. The compulsive connection between the two has often been attested even by those who have most strenuously repudiated the notion of 'theory' itself. Criticism of literature, Leavis after all proclaimed, is 'criticism of life'. This involuntary movement, stated or suggested, from the literary to the social has not so generally been reversed in a movement from the social to the literary. The reasons are not hard to seek. For literary criticism, whether 'practical' or 'theoretical', is typically just that, *criticism* — its irrepressibly *evaluative* impulse spontaneously tending to transgress the frontiers of the text towards the associated life beyond it. Social theory as such paradoxically lacks a comparable discriminatory charge built into it. The mainstream action theory that dominated North American sociology for so long is a case close to hand. Whereas most theories of literature propose, directly or obliquely, some discourse on society, the theories of society that contain, even indirectly, a discourse on literature are relatively few. It is difficult to imagine a Parsonian poetics; but it is easy enough to discern a sociology or a history at work in the New Criticism.

The critical theory which I am going to discuss is in this respect an exception. Marxism falls, of course, massively and pre-eminently into the category of those systems of thought concerned with the nature and direction of society as a whole. It has also, however, unlike most of its rivals in this field, developed an extensive discourse on literature in this century. There are a number of reasons for this, but one of them is no doubt to be found in the very intransigence of the *critique* which the founders of historical materialism made of the capitalist order in which they lived. Radically and inexpugnably critical in outlook from the start, Marxism was carried swiftly by its own impetus, as it were, onto the terrain of literary criticism. Marx's correspondence with Lassalle shows how natural this movement was, in its inaugural gesture. This is not to say that there was any easy concord between social and literary discourses within Marxism, then or later. On the contrary, the record of their relations has been a complex, tense and uneven one, riven by multiple breaks, displacements and deadlocks. If no complete rupture has ever occurred, since the days more or less of Mehring, it is doubtless due to the fact that beyond their common *critical* starting-point, there has always been an ultimate *historical* line of flight along the horizon of each. It is not entirely fortuitous, then, that the contemporary locution 'critical theory' should have two dominant connotations: on the one hand a generalized body of theory about literature, on the other a particular corpus of theory about society descending from Marx. It is the latter that customarily acquires capitals, a shift into upper case essentially effected by the Frankfurt School in the 1930s. Horkheimer, who codified this sense in 1937, intended to recover with it the sharp philosophical edge of Marx's materialism, unduly blunted — as his generation saw it — by the heritage of the Second International. Politically, Horkheimer declared, the 'only concern' of the critical theorist was to 'accelerate a development that should lead to a society without exploitation'.[1]

1. Max Horkheimer, 'Traditionelle und kritische Theorie', *Zeitschrift für Sozial-*

Intellectually, however, he sought – in Adorno's later words – 'to make men theoretically conscious of what it is that distinguishes materialism'.[2] The main thrust of the Frankfurt School's interventions over the years lay in just this direction — a long and passionate critical elucidation of the bequests and contradictions of classical philosophy and its contemporary successors, one which led increasingly, over the years, towards the domains of literature and art in the work of Adorno or Marcuse, each of whom brought their careers to rest in the realm of aesthetics. Still, to define Marxism as a critical theory simply in terms of the goal of a classless society, or the procedures of a consciously materialist philosophy, is obviously insufficient. The real propriety of the term for Marxism lies elsewhere.

What is distinctive about the kind of criticism that historical materialism in principle represents, is that it includes, indivisibly and unremittingly, *self*-criticism. That is, Marxism is a theory of history that lays claim, at the same stroke, to provide a history of the theory. A Marxism of Marxism was inscribed in its charter from the outset, when Marx and Engels defined the conditions of their own intellectual discoveries as the emergence of the determinate class contradictions of capitalist society itself, and their political objectives not merely as 'an ideal state of affairs', but as borne by the 'real movement of things'. This conception involved no element of complacent positivity — as if truth were henceforward guaranteed by time, Being by Becoming, their doctrine immune from error by mere immersion in change. 'Proletarian revolutions,' wrote Marx, 'criticize themselves constantly, interrupt themselves continually in their own course, come back to the apparently accomplished in order to begin it afresh, deride with unmerciful thoroughness the inadequacies, weaknesses and paltrinesses of their first attempts, seem to throw down their adversary only that he may draw new strength from the earth and rise again, more gigantic, before them.'[3] Two generations later Karl Korsch was the

forschung, Vol. 2, 1937, p.274. He went on to note that such a theorist could 'find himself in contradiction with views prevalent among the exploited' — indeed, 'without the possibility of that conflict there would be no need for the theory they require, since it would be immediately available'.

2. Theodor Adorno, *Negative Dialectics*, London 1973, p.197.

3. Karl Marx, 'The Eighteenth Brumaire of Louis Bonaparte', in Marx-Engels, *Selected Works*, Moscow 1951, p.228.

first to apply this revolutionary self-criticism to the development of Marxism since the heady days of 1848, distinguishing — as he put it — 'three major stages through which Marxist theory has passed *since* its birth — inevitably so in the context of the concrete social development of this epoch.'[4] These words were written in 1923. Without being altogether aware of it, their author was with them ushering in a fourth stage in the history of Marxist theory — one whose final shape was to be far from his expectations and hopes at the time. I have myself tried to explore something of what that shape proved to be, in an essay on the course and pattern of Western Marxism from the aftermath of the First World War to the end of the long boom that followed the Second World War — the half-century between 1918 and 1968.[5] That survey, written in the mid-seventies, included a diagnosis and some predictions. It sketched a provisional balance-sheet of a long period that seemed to be drawing to a close, and suggested other directions in which Marxist theory would or should move, in a new setting. A major purpose of these lectures will be to measure the accuracy of the analysis and the anticipations of that text, in the light of subsequent developments.

Before this task is tackled, however, it is necessary to make a preliminary observation. I have said that Marxism lies apart from all other variants of critical theory in its ability — or at least ambition — to compose a *self*-critical theory capable of explaining its own genesis and metamorphoses. This peculiarity needs some further specifications, however. We do not expect physics or biology to provide us with the concepts necessary to think their emergence as a science. Another vocabulary, anchored in a context that is conventionally distinguished as one of 'discovery' rather than 'validation', is needed for that purpose. To be sure, the principles of intelligibility of the history of these sciences are not simply external to them. On the contrary, the paradox is that, once constituted, they typically achieve a relatively high degree of immanent evolution, regulated by the respective problems posed within each and by their successive resolutions. What Georges Canguilhem, himself a historian of the life sciences conspicuously committed to the study of the 'normative'

4. Karl Korsch, *Marxism and Philosophy*, London 1970, p.51.
5. *Considerations on Western Marxism*, London 1976.

social dimensions impinging on them, nevertheless does not hesitate to call their common 'axiological activity, the quest for truth', [6] acts as an internal regulator increasingly, if far from completely, insulating them from a sheerly external order of determinations in cultural or political history. One might say that although the origins of the natural sciences escape their own theoretical field entirely, the further they develop the less need they have of any other theoretical field to explain their development. The institutionalized 'quest for truth', and the structure of problems set by the governing paradigm, suffice in predominant measure to account for their growth. Canguilhem, like Lakatos in the Anglo-Saxon philosophy of science, affirms in this sense the priority of the internal history of the concepts of the natural sciences, in their sequence of derivations, ruptures and transformations. For Canguilhem, their external history, always present, typically becomes causally crucial only at the junctures when 'normal' progress falters.

By contrast, disciplines like literary studies — traditionally described as the humanities — have rarely made any claim to cumulative rational progress of this sort. They fall subject to the same kind of external determinations in their origins, but never elude them in the same way thereafter. In other words, they possess neither axiological stability derived from the autonomy of the veridical, nor self-reflexive mobility capable of explaining their changing patterns of enquiry in terms of their own concepts. One discipline that explicitly sought to do the latter was, of course, the sociology of knowledge developed by Scheler and Mannheim. But its effort over-reached itself, ending in a relativism that effectively denied any cognitive validity to the ideologies or utopias it dismantled, thereby undermining its own pretensions. 'The "all" of the indiscriminately total concept of ideology,' Adorno remarked, 'terminates in nothingness. Once it has ceased to differ from any true consciousness it is no longer fit to criticize a false one.'[7] He rightly insisted that the dividing-line separating any such sociology of knowledge from historical materialism was the 'idea of objective truth'. We shall see the surprising importance of this apparently

6. Georges Canguilhem, *Etudes d'Histoire de Philosophie des Sciences*, Paris 1970, p.19.
   7. *Negative Dialectics*, p.198.

innocuous commonplace tomorrow. For the moment, it is merely necessary to point out that the protocols for a Marxist reflection on Marxism must therefore be twofold. On the one hand, the destiny of historical materialism in any given period must first of all be situated within the intricate web of national and international class struggles which characterize it, and whose course its own instruments of thought are designed to capture. Marxist theory, bent on understanding the world, has always aimed at an asymptotic unity with a popular practice seeking to transform it. The trajectory of the theory has thus always been *primarily* determined by the fate of that practice. Any report on the Marxism of the past decade will inevitably, then, be in the first instance a political history of its external environment. Parodying the slogan of the German historical school of Ranke, one might speak of a permanent *Primat der Aussenpolitik* in any responsible accounting of the development of historical materialism as a theory — in this respect, the very reverse of the order of priorities in Wellek and Warren's *Theory of Literature*, in which 'intrinsic' prevailed over 'extrinsic' approaches.[8] But at the same time, precisely because of all the distance that separates Marx from Mannheim (or his modern successors), such an accounting must also confront the *internal* obstacles, aporias, blockages of the theory in its own attempt to approximate to a general truth of the time. A purely reductive history of Marxism, flattening it out on the anvil of world politics, contradicts the nature of its object. There were socialists before Marx: the scandal he introduced, which still affronts many socialists — not to speak of capitalists — today, was the aspiration towards a *scientific* socialism: that is, one governed by rationally controllable criteria of evidence and truth. An *internal* history, of cognitive blindnesses and impediments, as well as advances or insights, is essential to a real scrutiny of the fortunes of Marxism in these past years, as of other ones. Without that, the stringency of genuine self-criticism would be absent: the recourse to the wider movement of history would tend to slip away from, or beyond, material explanation to intellectual exemption or exculpation.

8. René Wellek and Austin Warren, *Theory of Literature*, London 1963: compare pp.73-74 with 139-141.

Let us now pass to the matters in hand. The configuration of Western Marxism that held for so long after the victory and isolation of the Russian Revolution was — as I tried to describe it — fundamentally the product of the repeated defeats of the labour movement in the strongholds of advanced capitalism in continental Europe, after the first breakthrough by the Bolsheviks in 1917. Those defeats came in three waves: first, the proletarian insurgency in Central Europe immediately after the First World War — in Germany, Austria, Hungary, Italy — was beaten back between 1918 and 1922, so that fascism emerged triumphant in all these countries within a decade. Second, the Popular Fronts of the late thirties, in Spain and France, were undone with the fall of the Spanish Republic and the collapse of the Left in France that paved the way for Vichy two years later. Finally, the Resistance movements, led by mass Communist and Socialist parties, sputtered out across Western Europe in 1945-46, unable to translate their ascendancy in the armed struggle against Nazism into any durable political hegemony thereafter. The long post-war boom then gradually and inexorably subordinated labour to capital within the stabilized parliamentary democracies and emergent consumer societies of the OECD order.

It was within this overall set of historical coordinates that a new kind of Marxist theory crystallized. In the East, Stalinism was consolidated in the USSR. In the West, the oldest and largest capitalist societies in the world persisted undisturbed by any revolutionary challenges from below, in Britain and the United States. Between these two flanks, a post-classical form of Marxism flourished in those societies where the labour movement was strong enough to pose a genuine revolutionary threat to capital, incarnating a mass political practice that formed the necessary horizon of all socialist thought, yet was not strong enough actually to overthrow capital — undergoing, on the contrary, successive and radical defeats at each critical testing-point. Germany, Italy and France were the three major countries where Western Marxism found its homelands in the five decades between 1918 and 1968. The nature of this Marxism could not but bear the impress of the disasters that accompanied and surrounded it. Above all, it was marked by the sundering of the bonds that should have linked it to a popular movement for revolutionary socialism.

These had existed at the outset, as the careers of its trio of founding fathers show — Lukács, Korsch and Gramsci, each an active leader and organizer in the communist movement in his own country in the aftermath of the First World War. But as these pioneers ended in exile or prison, theory and practice drifted fatally apart, under the pressure of the time. The sites of Marxism as a discourse gradually became displaced from trade unions and political parties to research institutes and university departments. Inaugurated with the rise of the Frankfurt School in the late twenties and early thirties, the change was virtually absolute by the period of the High Cold War in the fifties, when there was scarcely a Marxist theoretician of any weight who was not the holder of a chair in the academy, rather than a post in the class struggle.

This shift of institutional terrain was reflected in an alteration of intellectual focus. Where Marx had successively moved from philosophy to politics to economics in his own studies, Western Marxism inverted his route. Major economic analyses of capitalism, within a Marxist framework, largely petered out after the Great Depression; political scanning of the bourgeois state dwindled away after the silencing of Gramsci; strategic discussion of the roads to a realizable socialism disappeared almost entirely. What increasingly took their place was a revival of *philosophical* discourse proper, itself centred on questions of method — that is, more epistemological than substantive in character. In this respect, Korsch's work of 1923, *Marxism and Philosophy*, proved prophetic. Sartre, Adorno, Althusser, Marcuse, Della Volpe, Lukács, Bloch and Colletti all produced major syntheses essentially focused on problems of cognition, however dialectically reformulated, written in an idiom of forbidding technical difficulty. For their purposes, each had recourse to philosophical legacies anterior to Marx himself: Hegel, Spinoza, Kant, Kierkegaard, Schelling or others. At the same time, each school within Western Marxism developed in close contact, often quasi-symbiosis, with coeval intellectual systems of a non-Marxist character; borrowing concepts and themes from Weber in the case of Lukács, Croce in the case of Gramsci, Heidegger in the case of Sartre, Lacan in the case of Althusser, Hjelmslev in that of Della Volpe, and so on. The patterning of this series of lateral relationships to bourgeois culture, alien to the tradition of classical Marxism, was itself a function of the dislocation of the relationships that had once held between it and the practice of the workers' movement. The lapse of these latter in turn inflected the whole Western Marxist tradition towards a subjacent pessimism, exhibited in the very innovations which it brought to the thematic range of historical materialism — whether in Sartre's theory of the logic of scarcity, Marcuse's vision of social one-dimensionality, Althusser's insistence on the permanence of ideological illusion, Benjamin's fear of the confiscation of the history of the past, or even Gramsci's own bleak stoicism.

At the same time, within its newly constricted parameters, the brilliance and fertility of this tradition were by any standards remarkable. Not merely did Marxist philosophy achieve a general plateau of sophistication far beyond its median levels of the past; but the major exponents of Western Marxism also typically pioneered studies of *cultural* processes — in the higher ranges of the superstructures — as if in glittering compensation for their neglect of the structures and infrastructures of politics and economics. Above all, art and ideology were the privileged terrain of much of this tradition, sounded by thinker after thinker with an imagination and precision that historical materialism had never deployed here before. In the final days of Western Marxism, one can, indeed, speak of a veritable hypertrophy of the aesthetic — which came to be surcharged with all the values that were repressed or denied elsewhere in the atrophy of living socialist politics: utopian images of the future, ethical maxims for the present, were displaced and condensed into the vaulting meditations on art with which Lukács or Adorno or Sartre concluded much of their life's work.

Still, whatever the outer limits of the tradition represented by theorists like these, in and through its very distance from immediate political practice it remained proof against any temptations to compromise with the established order. Western Marxism as a whole refused any reformist compact. The soil from which it arose was one in which mass Communist parties commanded the allegiance of the vanguard of the working class in the major countries of continental Europe — parties which by the late twenties were at once intransigent foes of capital, and Stalinized structures that permitted no serious discussion or dissent on major political issues, debarring in advance any revolutionary circuit between theory and practice. In these conditions, some of the major minds of Western Marxism — Lukács, Althusser, Della Volpe — chose to remain formal members of their respective parties, while developing as far as they could a discourse remote from official dogmas, in coded opposition to them. Others, like Sartre, attempted to theorize the practice of these parties from a position outside them. Others again, like Adorno in post-war Germany, abstained from any direct relationship to politics whatsoever. But none of these capitulated to the status quo, or ever embellished it, through the worst years of the Cold War.

This long and tantalizing tradition — so I argued — was finally becoming exhausted at the turn of the seventies. There were two reasons for that. The first was the reawakening of mass revolts within Western Europe — indeed right across the advanced capitalist world — where the great wave of student unrest in 1968 heralded the entry of massive contingents of the working class into a new political insurgency, of a kind not seen since the days of the Spartacists or the Turin councils. The May explosion in France was the most spectacular of these, followed by the tide of industrial militancy in Italy in 1969, the decisive miners' strike in Britain which overthrew the Conservative government in 1974, and then, a few months later, the upheaval in Portugal, with its rapid radicalization towards a revolutionary situation of the most classic type. In none of these cases did the impetus for popular rebellion derive from the established parties of the Left, whether Social-Democratic or Communist. What they appeared to prefigure was the possibility of an end to the semi-secular divorce of socialist theory from mass working-class practice, which had left such a crippling mark on Western Marxism itself. At the same time, the protracted post-war boom came to an abrupt halt in 1974, for the first time in 25 years putting the basic socio-economic stability of advanced capitalism in question. Subjectively and objectively, then, conditions seemed to be clearing the way for another sort of Marxism to emerge.

My own conclusions as to its likely shape — conclusions that were also recommendations, lived in a spirit of reasoned optimism — were fourfold. Firstly, I reckoned that the surviving doyens of the Western

Marxist tradition were unlikely to produce any further work of significant moment, while many of their immediate disciples were showing signs of veering towards what would be a disastrous fixation with China as an alternative model of post-revolutionary society to the USSR, and an exemplar for socialist explorations in the West. Secondly, I suggested that the reopening of a loop between Marxist theory and mass practice in the advanced countries could recreate some of the conditions that had once formed the classical canon of historical materialism in the generation of Lenin or Luxemburg. Any such reunification of theory and practice would have two consequences, I thought: it would inevitably shift the whole centre of gravity of Marxist culture towards the set of basic problems posed by the movement of the world economy, the structure of the capitalist state, the constellation of social classes, the meaning and function of the nation — all of which had been systematically neglected for many years. A turn to the concrete, a *return* to the preoccupations of the mature Marx or Lenin, seemed to impose itself. Such a change would necessarily revive that dimension which above all else had been missing from the Western Marxist tradition since the death of Gramsci — namely, *strategic* discussion of the ways in which a revolutionary movement could break past the barriers of the bourgeois-democratic state to a real socialist democracy beyond it. Once there was any renewal of strategic debate, I speculated, it was likely that the major oppositional tradition to Stalinism that had survived in direct, if radically marginalized, continuity from classical Marxism — that which descended from Trotsky — would tend to acquire a new relevance and vitality, freed from the conservatism in which its defence of a vanquished past had often tended to congeal it.

Thirdly, I predicted that any renascence of a more classical cast of Marxist culture would be virtually bound to involve the spread of the latter to the Anglo-American bastions of imperialism, which by and large had resisted historical materialism so successfully in the epoch of 'Western' Marxism itself. It was in the UK and USA, after all — the oldest and the most powerful of capitalist states, respectively — that the most testing problems for socialist theory had always been posed, and left perforce unanswered. The campus revolts of the late sixties, whatever their other limitations, appeared to hold the promise of a future socialist intelligentsia capable of surpassing in quantity and quality anything either society had known in the past. Fourthly, and finally, I argued that any further development of historical materialism would not only have to re-examine, tranquilly and firmly, the heritage of the classical thinkers, from Marx and Engels through to Lenin, Luxemburg and Trotsky, seeking to identify, criticize and resolve their characteristic omissions or confusions. It would also have to come to terms with the fundamental gains made by Marxist *historiography* — above all in the Anglo-American area — since the Second World War, which had hitherto always lain outside the central perimeter of Marxist *theory*, dominated as it was by the discipline of philosophy. The confrontation and integration of the two would involve a reconsideration of the whole statute and significance of the *past*, in a system of thought geared overwhelmingly, at a day-to-day level, to the present or future; and it would leave neither history nor theory unchanged in the encounter between the two.[9]

Such were my conjectures at the time. How have they fared, against the actual course of events? Their most general surmise, it seems to me, has been confirmed — though, as we shall see, in a way that gives no cause for comfort or complacency. That is to say, the grand Western Marxist tradition — with its epistemological or aesthetic, sombre or esoteric tonalities — has effectively come to an end, and in its stead there has emerged, with remarkable celerity and confidence, another kind of Marxist culture, primarily oriented towards just those questions of an economic, social or political order that had been lacking from its predecessor. The productivity of this Marxism has been formidable, leaving little doubt that we have been witnessing a period of overall growth and emancipation. Within this broad perspective, however, history had — as usual — prepared some disconcerting surprises and ironies for the guesses hazarded at the time. Let us look at this in more detail.

The conviction that the Western Marxist tradition had essentially run its course was, as I have said, proved correct. This was not an especially difficult development to foresee. In part, the sheer bio-

9. See *Considerations on Western Marxism* pp. 101-102; 95-101; 102-103; 109-112.

logical toll of the generation of elders was bound to play its part. Between the watershed year of 1968 and the time of my essay, death caught up with Della Volpe, Adorno, Goldmann, Lukács and Horkheimer. By the end of the decade Bloch, Marcuse and Sartre had followed. But the process of exhaustion at work had other sources as well. The two youngest of the theorists I had discussed were Althusser and Colletti, both of whom were still in their prime in these years. Yet, much as anticipated, neither produced any work of substance thereafter, declining into repetition or denegation. By and large, a line could be drawn below the original Western Marxist experience by the middle of the seventies.

What succeeded it? A sudden zest, a new appetite, for the concrete. If we pass in review those key topics which had remained most ignored by the Western Marxist tradition, and on whose enumeration I had insisted in 1974, we can see that in the majority of cases they brought forth concentrated theoretical activity, often yielding notable syntheses, in the next years. The laws of motion of the capitalist mode of production as a whole — which, if we except Baran and Sweezy's *Monopoly Capital*, with its quasi-Keynesian framework, had been fallow ground for Marxist enquiry since Grossmann's theorization on the eve of the Great Depression — were now explored by three decisive bodies of work: firstly, Ernest Mandel's path-breaking *Late Capitalism*, followed by his studies on *The Second Slump* and *Long Waves in the History of Capitalism*; secondly, Harry Braverman's great book on the transformation of the labour process in the twentieth century, *Labor and Monopoly Capital*; and thirdly, the French economist Michel Aglietta's ambitious and original *Theory of Capitalist Regulation*.[10] With works like these, Marxist discussion of contemporary capitalism has once again reached, and in some vital respects surpassed, the level of the classical epoch of Luxemburg and Hilferding. Concrete historical investigations have at the same time been accompanied by a renewal of intense conceptual and methodological debate, associated with the names of Morishima, Steedman,

10. Ernest Mandel, *Late Capitalism* (London 1975), *The Second Slump* (London 1978), *Long Waves of Capitalist Development — The Marxist Interpretation*, (Cambridge 1978); Harry Braverman, *Labor and Monopoly Capital*, New York 1975; Michel Aglietta, *A Theory of Capitalist Regulation: the US Experience*, London 1979.

Roemer, Lippi, Krause and others.[11] As to the political domain, the specific structures of the modern capitalist state had been one of the great blind areas of Western Marxism, all too little concerned with the precise nature of the *Western* polities in which it subsisted. Today, this absence too has in considerable measure been made good, with a series of important and cumulative studies. These include, of course, the five books by Nicos Poulantzas, exploring the whole gamut of parliamentary, fascist and military types of capitalist state; the more empirically based work of Ralph Miliband in England; the debates of the *Kapitallogik* school in West Germany, and the contributions of Claus Offe; and the pivotal recent book by the Swedish sociologist Göran Therborn *What does the Ruling Class do When it Rules?*.[12] At the same time, the new types of social stratification in late capitalism have been the object of studies at once more rigorous and more imaginative than anything historical materialism, even in its classical epoch, had produced in the past: Erik Olin Wright's work in the United States, that of the Italian Carchedi, and the investigations of Roger Establet and Christian Baudelot in France, have been outstanding in this regard.[13] The nature and dynamics of the post-capitalist states in the East, long prohibited terrain for serene enquiry on much of the European Left, have received new and searching attention, above all in Rudolf Bahro's extraordinary *The Alternative in Eastern Europe*, but also in more

11. See Michio Morishima, *Marx's Economics*, Cambridge 1973; Ian Steedman, *Marx After Sraffa*, London 1977; John Roemer, *A General Theory of Exploitation and Class*, Cambridge Mass., 1982; Marco Lippi, *Value and Naturalism in Marx*, London 1979; Ulrich Krause, *Money and Abstract Labour*, London 1982.

12. Nicos Poulantzas, *Political Power and Social Classes*, (London 1973), *Fascism and Dictatorship* (London 1974), *Classes and Contemporary Capitalism* (London 1975), *The Crisis of the Dictatorships* (London 1976), *State, Power, Socialism* (London 1978); Ralph Miliband, *The State in Capitalist Society* (London 1969), *Marxism and Politics* (Oxford 1977), *Capitalist Democracy in Britain* (Oxford 1982); John Holloway and Sol Picciotto, eds. *State and Capital*, London 1978; Claus Offe, *Strukturprobleme des kapitalistischen Staates*, Frankfurt 1975; Göran Therborn, *What Does the Ruling Class Do When It Rules? — State Apparatuses and State Power under Feudalism, Capitalism and Socialism*, London 1978: see also his important ensuing work, *The Ideology of Power and the Power of Ideology*, London 1980.

13. Erik Olin Wright, *Class, Crisis and the State*, (London 1978), and *Class Structure and Income Determination*, (New York 1979); Guglielmo Carchedi, *On the Economic Identification of Social Classes*, London 1977; Christian Baudelot and Roger Establet, *L'Ecole Capitaliste en France*, Paris 1971; (with Jacques Malemort), *La Petite Bourgeoisie en France*, Paris 1974; (with Jacques Toisier), *Qui Travaille pour Qui?*, Paris 1979.

specialist and scholarly form in the studies of economists like Nuti and Brus.[14] Nor has this expansion of Marxist theory in economics, politics and sociology been accompanied by any corresponding contraction in the fields of philosophy or culture — the peculiar vineyards of Western Marxism. On the contrary, these years have also seen the accumulating work of Raymond Williams in England, materialist cultural studies in their broadest sense, and of Fredric Jameson in the United States, in the more specifically literary domain; while in philosophy G. A. Cohen's *Karl Marx's Theory of History — A Defence*, bringing for the first time the procedural standards of analytic philosophy to bear on the basic concepts of historical materialism, is clearly the landmark of the decade.[15]

A staccato bibliography of this sort does not, of course, come near a comprehensive, let alone critical, inventory of the Marxist production of the past years. There are other works and names that could equally be mentioned; and those that have been are as much subject to their own limiting judgements as are any of their predecessors. However, even this rapid shorthand for a complex set of intellectual changes, which need much finer discrimination than there is time for here, indicates certain points. Although we can speak of a real topographical 'break' between Western Marxism and the emergent formation I have been outlining, in other respects there has perhaps been more continuity of connections than I allowed for, even if it has typically been a mediate one. Thus the influence of most of the older schools can be discerned in the background of many of the newcomers. The Althusserian current has probably persisted most strongly: of the names I mentioned earlier, Poulantzas, Therborn, Aglietta, Wright and Establet all owe different debts to it. The legacy of the Frankfurt School can be seen in Braverman's work, through Baran, and Offe's, through Habermas. The Lukácsian strain remains avowedly dominant in Jameson's work. Carchedi's reveals Della Volpean overtones. But

14. Rudolf Bahro, *The Alternative in Eastern Europe*, London 1978; Domenico Mario Nuti, 'The Contradictions of Socialist Economics', *The Socialist Register 1979;* Wlodzimierz Brus, *Socialist Ownership and Political Systems*, London 1975.
15. See Raymond Williams, *The Country and the City* (London 1973), *Marxism and Literature* (Oxford 1977), *Politics and Letters* (London 1979), *Problems in Materialism and Culture* (London 1980), *Culture* (London 1981); Fredric Jameson, *The Political Unconscious*, Ithaca 1981; G.A. Cohen, *Karl Marx's Theory of History — A Defence*, Oxford 1978.

at the same time, the very distribution of these authors hints at the more important fact that the geographical pattern of Marxist theory has been profoundly altered in the past decade. Today the *predominant* centres of intellectual production seem to lie in the English-speaking world, rather than in Germanic or Latin Europe. as was the case in the inter-war and post-war periods respectively. That shift in locus represents an arresting historical change. Very much as I had felt might happen, the traditionally most backward zones of the capitalist world, in Marxist culture, have suddenly become in many ways the most advanced.

A more extended survey of authors and works would bring this home fully: the sheer density of ongoing economic, political, sociological and cultural research on the Marxist Left in Britain or North America, with its undergrowth of journals and discussions, eclipses any equivalent in the older lands of the Western Marxist tradition proper. But there is, of course, a further reason for the nascent Anglo-American hegemony in historical materialism today — one that has in its turn verified another of the predictions made in the mid-seventies. That is the rise of Marxist historiography to its long overdue salience within the landscape of socialist thought as a whole. In this area, the dominance of English-speaking practitioners had been evident ever since the fifties, and for many decades Marxism as an intellectual force, at least in England, had been virtually synonymous with the work of historians. Even the one outstanding thinker of an older generation and another formation, the economist Maurice Dobb, characteristically achieved his greatest influence with the essentially historical *Studies in the Development of Capitalism* (published in 1947), stretching from the late Middle Ages to the modern corporation, rather than with his prolific output on Marx's political economy as such. It was Dobb's younger colleagues, gathered in the seminal Communist Party Historians' Group of the late forties and early fifties, however, who matured into the brilliant pleiad of scholars that transformed so many accepted interpretations of the English and European past in the following years: Christopher Hill, Eric Hobsbawm, Edward Thompson, George Rudé, Rodney Hilton, Victor Kiernan, Geoffrey de Ste-Croix and others. Most of these were publishing from the turn of the sixties onwards. But the consolidation of their collective work into a canon of commanding weight well beyond their own formal discipline, was really a development of the seventies. This was the decade which saw the publication of *The Age of Capital* by Hobsbawm, *The World Turned Upside Down* and *Milton and English Revolution* by Hill, *Bond Men Made Free* and *The English Peasantry in the Later Middle Ages* by Hilton, *Class Struggle and the Industrial Revolution* by Foster, *Whigs and Hunters* by Thompson, *Lords of Humankind* by Kiernan, now followed by Ste-Croix's monumental *Class Struggle in the Ancient Greek World*.[16] Perhaps Raymond Williams's most original and powerful book, *The Country and the City*, has its primary affiliation here, too. For someone of my generation, formed at a time when British culture seemed utterly barren of any indigenous Marxist impulse of moment, the laggard of Europe, which we constantly denounced as such, at risk of charges of 'national nihilism', this has been a truly astonishing metamorphosis. The traditional relationship between Britain and Continental Europe appears for the moment to have been effectively reversed — Marxist culture in the UK for the moment proving more productive and original than that of any mainland state.

Meanwhile, a more restricted but not dissimilar change has occurred in North America. Here too, historiography has been the leading sector, with an extremely rich range of work — not confined to American history itself — from Eugene Genovese, Eric Foner, David Montgomery, Robert Brenner, David Abraham and many others.[17]

16. Dates: *The Age of Capital*, London 1975; *The World Turned Upside Down*, London 1975; *Milton and the English Revolution*, London 1977; *Bond Men Made Free*, London 1973; *The English Peasantry in the Later Middle Ages*, Oxford 1975; *Class Struggle and the Industrial Revolution*, London 1974; *Whigs and Hunters*, London 1975; *Lords of Humankind*, London 1972; *The Class Struggle in the Ancient Greek World*, London 1981.

17. Eugene Genovese, *Roll, Jordan, Roll — The World the Slaves Made*, New York 1974, and *From Rebellion to Revolution: Afro-American Slave Revolts in the Making of the Modern World*, New York 1979; Eric Foner, *Free Soil, Free Labor, Free Men*, New York 1970, and *Tom Paine and Revolutionary America*, New York 1976; David Montgomery, *Beyond Equality: Labor and the Radical Republicans*, New York 1967, and *Workers' Control in America*, New York 1979; Robert Brenner, 'Agrarian Class Structure and Economic Development in Pre-Industrial Europe', and 'The Agrarian Roots of European Capitalism' *Past and Present*, No. 70, February 1976 and No. 97, November 1982; David Abraham, *The Collapse of the Weimar Republic: Political Economy and Crisis*, Princeton 1981.

But around it a broader socialist culture has developed, not all of it Marxist, of striking variety and vitality, from the historical sociology of Immanuel Wallerstein and Theda Skocpol to the political economy of James O'Connor, the continuing work of Paul Sweezy and Harry Magdoff, the cultural criticism of Christopher Lasch.[18] The panorama in this respect is today radically distinct from anything even imaginable fifteen years ago. It is one in which *Business Week* can lament the widespread penetration of historical materialism into US campuses only four short years after *Time* was proclaiming that Marx was finally dead, and handbooks can be produced on the Left simply to guide the curious student through the thickets — now passably luxuriant — of 'Marxism in the Academy', to paraphrase a recent title.[19]

This historically centred Marxist culture that has emerged in the Anglophone world has, finally, not remained confined to its own provinces. The theoretical juncture between historiography and philosophy to which I looked forward in the mid-seventies did punctually occur, if with a violence that was far from my expectation of it. Edward Thompson's prolonged and passionate polemic with Louis Althusser, *The Poverty of Theory*, turned an intellectual page — irreversibly. Whatever our view of the merits of the dispute, it is henceforward impossible for Marxists to proceed — as they did for many years, on either side — as if their history and their theory were two separate mental worlds, with little more than occasional tourism, mildly curious, between them. Theory now is history, with a seriousness and severity it never was in the past; as history is equally theory, in all its exigency, in a way that it typically evaded before. The assault by Thompson on Althusser also exemplified the breaking down of one further, crucial barrier: that which had always confined the major schools or debates within Western Marxism to *national* contexts, ensuring mutual ignorance or silence between them, to the detriment

18. Immanuel Wallerstein, *The Modern World System*, Vols. I and II, New York 1974 and 1980; Theda Skocpol, *States and Social Revolutions*, Cambridge 1979; James O'Connor, *The Fiscal Crisis of the State*, New York 1973; Harry Magdoff and Paul Sweezy, *The Deepening Crisis of US Capitalism*, New York 1981; Christopher Lasch, *The Culture of Narcissism*, New York 1978.

19. Bertell Ollman and Edward Vernhoff, eds. *The Left Academy: Marxist Scholarship on American Campuses*, New York 1982.

of any genuinely internationalist discourse. This twofold gain — the new exchanges between history and theory, and across national frontiers — has been among the most fruitful changes in the past decade. That they are not mere swallows without a summer can be seen from the kindred styles of debate over the work of Immanuel Wallerstein on the world capitalist system, probed in essentially theoretical terms by Robert Brenner among others, and over the work of Brenner on the transition to capitalism, in its turn — the focus of one of the widest professional controversies since the war, with international responses from historians in Germany and France, England and Poland.[20] Similarly, the discussion of value theory in Marxist economics no longer has national boundaries, even of a temporary sort: the circuits of argument switch freely from Japan to Belgium, Canada to Italy, Britain to Germany or the US, as recent symposia testify.[21]

So far, then, the hopes and hypotheses advanced in my *Considerations on Western Marxism* seem to have been largely realized. But any note of satisfaction, let alone self-satisfaction, would be out of place. For in one absolutely decisive respect the flow of theory in these years did not run in the direction I had envisaged. The reunification of Marxist theory and popular practice in a mass revolutionary movement signally failed to materialize. The *intellectual* consequence of this failure was, logically and fatally, the general dearth of real *strategic* thinking on the Left in the advanced countries — that is, any elaboration of a concrete or plausible perspective for a transition beyond capitalist democracy to a socialist democracy. Rather than a

20. See Robert Brenner, 'The Origins of Capitalist Development: A Critique of Neo-Smithian Marxism', *New Left Review*, No. 104, July-August 1977, and the symposium on Brenner's work in *Past and Present* Nos. 78-80 and 85, February-August 1978 and November 1979, with contributions by Michael Postan and John Hatcher, Patricia Croot and David Parker, Heidi Wunder, Emmanuel Leroy Ladurie, Guy Bois, J.P. Cooper and Arnost Klima, now collected together with Brenner's formidable response, in *The Brenner Debate — Agrarian Class Structure and Economic Development in Pre-Industrial Europe*, Cambridge 1983 (forthcoming).

21. *The Value Controversy*, London 1981, with contributions from Ian Steedman, Paul Sweezy, Erik Olin Wright, Geoff Hodgson, Pradeep Bandyopadhyay, Makoto Itoh, Michel De Vroey, G.A. Cohen, Susan Himmelweit and Simon Mohun, and Anwar Shaikh.

'poverty of theory', what the Marxism that succeeded Western Marxism continues to share with its predecessor is a 'poverty of strategy'. It is impossible to point out any single body of writing in these years which reveals, even faintly, the kind of conceptual attack, the combination of political resolution and theoretical imagination that marked the great interventions of Luxemburg or Lenin, Trotsky or Parvus, in the years before the First World War. The determinants of this central deficit, which precludes any triumphalist retrospect of the past decade, pose the question of the larger social conditions in which Marxism developed in these years. But before we look at this wider historical context, it is necessary to take stock of a phenomenon whose ultimate relation to the strategic void remains to be ascertained, but whose immediate reality seems in the most clamorous contradiction to any claim for a renaissance of historical materialism in the seventies. I refer, of course, to what came to be called — among those most affected by, or interested in, it — the 'crisis of Marxism'. This process gave rise to the exultant covers of American and European mass media in 1977, of which *Time* magazine was only one. But although the scale and speed of the phenomenon were dramatic enough, the term itself was always a misleading one. What was really at issue was the crisis of a certain Marxism, geographically confined to Latin Europe — essentially France, Italy and Spain. Within this cultural and political area, there was indeed something approaching a collapse of the Marxist tradition by the late seventies, at the very moment when Marxism was conquering or consolidating new positions across a wide front outside it. It would be foolish to underestimate the gravity of this rout, not only for the countries concerned, but for the general credit of a rational socialist culture as a whole.

What were the characteristic syndromes of this crisis of Latin Marxism? Two major patterns can be distinguished. On the one hand, amidst a recrudescence of violent anti-communist fevers in the surrounding capitalist polity, in France and Italy especially, there was an abrupt and widespread renunciation of Marxism altogether, by thinkers of older and younger generations on the Left alike. The most spectacular reversal in this respect was perhaps that of Lucio Colletti, once the foremost Marxist philosopher in Italy, who in the space of three or four years became a shrill enemy of Marxism and staunch defender of a more or less conventional liberalism. His most recent book is not inappropriately entitled *The Passing Away Of Ideology*,[23] in unconscious reminiscence of a celebrated text in American sociology of some twenty years ago. In France, Sartre in his last years followed his own trajectory from denunciation of communism to formal renunciation of Marxism, in his case in the name of a radical neo-anarchism.[24] The mutation, or decline, of these eminences was no isolated affair, however. It corresponded to a much wider change of mood in literary and philosophical circles once associated with the Left. Emblematic in this regard were the writers and critics of the *Tel Quel* group, Philippe Sollers, Julia Kristeva and others, who switched virtually overnight from strident asseverations of materialism and a cult of the social order in China, to revaluations of mysticism and exaltation of the social order in the United States.[25] André Glucksmann, barricade rebel and intellectual protegé of Louis Althusser in the late sixties, became the leading publicist of the 'New' Philosophy — that is, a reiteration of the oldest themes in the ideological arsenal of the Cold War in the fifties, such as the equation of Marxism with totalitarianism, the identification of socialism with Stalinism.

Meanwhile, there was a second type of response to the change in political temperature in Latin Europe in the late seventies. This was not so much an outright repudiation or relinquishment of Marxism, as a dilution or diminution of it, pervaded by an increasing scepticism towards the very idea of a revolutionary rupture with capitalism. Symptomatic of this trend was Althusser's growing distance from the political legacy of historical materialism as such, expressed in the denial that it had ever possessed any theory of State or politics, and betokening a radical loss of morale in one whose assertions of the

23. *Tramonto dell'Ideologia*, Rome 1980.
24. See the interviews given to *Lotta Continua*, 15 September 1977, and to *Le Nouvel Observateur*, 10-30 March 1980 (under the title 'L'Espoir Maintenant'). The latter was published on the eve of his death, after the long loss of his physical powers so painfully recorded by Simone De Beauvoir, who views the text as a distorted mirror, the work of a manipulative interviewer, which she criticized to Sartre at the time. These circumstances qualify, but do not cancel, the changed direction of his final years. See Simone De Beauvoir, *La Céremonie des Adieux*, Paris 1981, pp. 149-152.
25. See, inter alia, Julia Kristeva, Marcelin Pleynet and Philippe Sollers, *Pourquoi les Etats-Unis?*, the special number of *Tel Quel* devoted to the United States, No. 71-73, Autumn 1977.

scientific supremacy of Marxism had been more overweening and categorical than those of any other theorist of his time. Soon it was Althusser who was propagating the notion of 'a general crisis of Marxism' — a crisis he showed little haste to resolve.[26] Poulantzas, for his part, once a pillar of Leninist rectitude, now rediscovered the virtues of parliaments and the dangers of dual power: his final interviews before his death spoke, beyond even these, of a crisis of confidence in 'politics' as such.[27] The shadow of Michel Foucault, soon proclaiming the 'end of politics'[28] as Bell or Colletti had done of ideology, no doubt lay heavily on these Parisian doubts. In Italy, the Communist Party itself was increasingly rife with similar currents. Its leading younger philosopher, Massimo Cacciari, told Italian workers from his chair in the Chamber of Deputies that Nietzsche had outdated Marx, the will to power proving more fundamental than the class struggle; while a sometimes sympathetic interest in the ideas of Friedman or Bentham could be found among many of his colleagues.

No intellectual change is ever universal. At least one exception, of signal honour, stands out against the general shift of positions in these years. The oldest living survivor of the Western Marxist tradition I discussed, Henri Lefebvre, neither bent nor turned in his eighth decade, continuing to produce imperturbable and original work on subjects typically ignored by much of the Left.[29] The price of such constancy, however, was relative isolation. Surveying the intellectual scene as a whole, we are left with an uncanny paradox. At the very time when Marxism as a critical theory has been in unprecedented ascent in the English-speaking world, it has undergone a precipitous descent in the Latin societies where it was most powerful and productive in the post-war period. In France and Italy above all, the two leading homelands of a living historical materialism in the fifties and sixties, for anyone like myself who learnt much of their Marxism from these cultures, the massacre of ancestors has been impressive.

26. See 'The Crisis of Marxism', *Marxism Today*, July 1978.

27. See the interview 'Le Risposte che è Difficile Trovare', *Rinascita*, 12 October 1979.

28. See the interview, conducted by Bernard-Henri Lévy, with Foucault on the *History of Sexuality*, in *Le Nouvel Observateur*, No. 644, 12 March 1977.

29. Of especial interest are his works on urbanism: *Le Droit à la Ville*, Paris 1967, and *La Production de l'Espace*, Paris 1974.

What is its meaning? The transverse movements of Marxist theory in the past decade remain to be explored. The problems they pose will be our topic tomorrow.

2
Structure and Subject

The rough cadastral survey of the present state of Marxist theory attempted yesterday ended with a conundrum: that is, the abrupt subsidence — in some respects, to the point of collapse — of historical materialism as an active and productive culture in France and Italy, in a period when elsewhere in the advanced capitalist world it was shaping a new intellectual landscape. Today, I wish to explore some alternative hypotheses that might throw light on the character and causes of this Latin recession within the international map of contemporary Marxism. In doing so, I will confine myself essentially to its French dimension. This involves no basic limitation, I think, because Italian - and *a fortiori* Spanish — culture has since the war been increasingly subject to directions and emphases derived from Paris, even if these have always been qualified and mediated by others coming from Germany: the inter-section of the two, indeed, defining much of the area of debate in Italian philosophy. More: in the three decades or so after the Liberation, France came to enjoy a cosmopolitan paramountcy in the general Marxist universe that recalls in its own way something of the French ascendancy in the epoch of the Enlightenment. The fall of this dominance in the later seventies was thus no mere national matter. We have registered some of the symptoms of that fall — the veritable *débandade* of so many leading French thinkers of the Left since 1976. Its consequences have been drastic. Paris today is the capital of European intellectual reaction, in much the same way that London was thirty years ago. Our question, however, is: what were the *causes* of this historic local defeat of historical materialism?

I argued earlier that Marxism, as a criticial theory aspiring to provide the reflexive intelligibility of its own development, accords in principle a priority to extrinsic explanations of its successes, failures or impasses. At the same time, I stressed that this is never an absolute or exclusive primacy, of a kind that would exempt the theory from any ultimate responsibilities. On the contrary, the complementary necessity of an *internal* history of the theory, measuring its vitality as a research programme governed by the quest for truth characteristic of any rational knowledge, is what separates Marxism from any variant of pragmatism or relativism. In looking at the problem posed by the demoralization and retreat of Gallic Marxism, therefore, I will start by considering a hypothesis that relates to its intrinsic evolution first. The hypothesis is simply this: that after French Marxism had enjoyed a lengthy period of largely uncontested cultural dominance, basking in the remote, reflected prestige of the Liberation, it finally encountered an intellectual adversary that was capable of doing battle with it, and prevailing. Its victorious opponent was the broad theoretical front of structuralism, and then its post-structuralist successors. The crises of Latin Marxism, then, would be the result, not of a circumstantial decline, but of a head-on defeat. The evidence of that defeat, it could be argued, is the triumphant ascendancy of structuralist or post-structuralist ideas and themes wherever Marxist ones once held sway — a virtually 'epistemic' shift of the type Michel Foucault sought to theorize.

The plausibility of this hypothesis is reinforced by a further consideration. Unlike in this respect the mysteriously abrupt and total changes from one cognitive 'pediment' to another (Foucault) or one 'problematic' to the next (Althusser), the passage from Marxist to structuralist and then post-structuralist dominants in post-war French culture has not involved a complete discontinuity of issues or questions. On the contrary, it is clear that there has been one master-problem around which *all* contenders have revolved; and it would look as if it was precisely the superiority of — in the first instance — structuralism on *the very terrain* of Marxism itself that assured it of decisive victory over the latter. What was this problem? Essentially, the nature of the relationships between structure and subject in human history and society. Now, the enigma of the respective status and position of these two was not a marginal or local area of uncertainty in Marxist theory. Indeed, it has always constituted one of the most central and fundamental problems of historical materialism as an account of the development of human civilization. We can see this immediately if we reflect on the permanent oscillation, the potential disjuncture in Marx's own writings between his ascription of the primary motor of historical change to the contradiction between the forces of production and the relations of production, on the one hand — think of the famous 1859 'Introduction' to the *Contribution to the Critique of Political Economy*; and to the class struggle, on the other hand — think of *The Communist Manifesto*. The first refers essentially to a structural, or more properly inter-structural, reality: the order of what contemporary sociology would call system integration (or for Marx, latent disintegration). The second refers to the subjective forces contending and colliding for mastery over social forms and historical processes: the realm of what contemporary sociology would call social integration (that is equally disintegration or reintegration). How are these two distinct types of causality, or principles of explanation, to be articulated in the theory of historical materialism?

On this score, classical Marxism, even at the height of its powers, provided no coherent answer. The political antinomies to which the persistent elusion or suspension of the question gave rise were, of course, widely and passionately debated: economism on the one side, voluntarism on the other. Lenin's pre-war interventions can be seen as a constant effort to control and combat these two possible deductions from Marx's legacy — whose political expressions were the contrasting tendencies towards reformism and anarchism, on the Right and far Left of the Second International respectively. But these interventions remained purely practical and conjunctural, without theoretical foundation. The same unresolved issues have haunted Marxist historiography as much as Marxist politics. The extensive contemporary discussion of Edward Thompson's work, for example, has largely focused on the role of human agency in the making or unmaking of classes, and the advent or supersession of social structures, whether of industrial capitalism or a socialism beyond it. Another particularly eloquent case in which this problem lies at the root of the differences between two major, rival Marxist interpretations of the same historical process can be found in Robert Brenner's and Guy Bois's counter-construals of the epochal transition from feudalism to agrarian capitalism in early modern Europe — the one axed essentially on the variable correlation of class forces in the late mediaeval countryside, the other on the invariant logic of falling rates of seigneurial rent in the feudal economy.[1]

For our purposes here, the relevant point is that this inveterate tension — at times lesion — within historical materialism took neither a directly political nor a historiographic form in post-war France. Rather, it emerged as the central problem investing the field of *philosophy*. The reasons for this lay essentially in the overall configuration of the years after the Liberation. The political scene on the Left was dominated by the massive, adamantine presence of the French Communist Party, without contest the major organization of the working class and the major threat to the French bourgeoisie, yet at the same time a rigidly bureaucratized command system that precluded any theoretical debate or discourse of a Bolshevik type on its own strategy. The historical profession, on the other hand, was soon under the sway of the *Annales* school, then progressive in its social sympathies, but intellectually not only very distant from Marxism but largely uninterested in the problem of agency as such, which it identified with mere surface events, in its pursuit of deeper processes or longer durations in history. On the other hand, the most influential philosophical formation was phenomenological and existentialist in its pre-war origins, with roots in Kojeve, Husserl and Heidegger. As such as it was an accentuated, even exasperated, ontology of the subject. Yet it was aligned on the Left, and now sought to come to terms with the structural reality of the Communist Party in front of it, at a time of turbulent class struggles in France. The result was the sustained attempt to rethink the relations between subject and structure, in the form of some synthesis between Marxism and existentialism, undertaken by Sartre, Merleau-Ponty and De Beauvoir in the late forties and early fifties. The debates that divided them in this initially common enterprise were of a rare quality and intensity, forming one of the richest episodes in the intellectual history of the post-war epoch as a whole. Although primarily determined by the

1. See the exchange in *The Brenner Debate*, and for Bois's position more generally, his *Crise du Féodalisme*, Paris 1976.

divergence of their political judgements and epistemological starting-points, these debates also reflected horizons in the social sciences in France at the time: Merleau-Ponty was a reader of Weber, Sartre of Braudel. Their culmination was, of course, the publication of Sartre's *Critique of Dialectical Reason* in 1960 — a work which was initially conceived as a direct response to the criticisms and objections put to him by Merleau-Ponty during their famous exchanges in the mid-fifties, and whose exclusive theme is the labyrinth of interversions between praxis and process, individuals and groups, groups and the practico-inert, in a history unleashed and pervaded by scarcity.

It is important to recollect that Sartre's *Critique* prefaced a 600-page 'Theory of Practical Ensembles' with a short essay, 'The Question of Method', that had initially been published in 1957. For although their author described their common aim as the constitution of a 'historical, structural anthropology', their focus in fact significantly differed. *The Question of Method* was essentially concerned with the theoretical instruments necessary to understand the total meaning of the life of an individual, as what Sartre called a 'singular universal', proposing the integration of Marxist, psychoanalytic and sociological concepts in a unitary interpretative method. It pointed towards biography. The *Critique* proper, on the other hand, aimed to provide a philosophical account of the 'elementary formal structures' of any possible history, or a theory of the general mechanisms of the construction and sub-version of all social groups. History itself, the 'diachronic totalization' of all these 'practical multiplicities, and of all their struggles',[2] was to be the object of a promised second volume. In other words, the horizon of the *Critique* was an attempt to understand not the truth of one person but — as Sartre put it — 'the truth of humanity as a whole' (even if, for him, there was a basic epistemological continuity between the two). It pointed towards a global history, whose declared terminus would be a totalizing comprehension of the meaning of the contem-porary epoch. This, the largest promise that perhaps any writer has ever given in the twentieth century, was not to be kept. Sartre wrote a second volume equal in length to the first, but abandoned it unfinished

2. *Critique of Dialectical Reason*, London 1976, pp.817, 822.

and unpublished. In that pregnant act of desistance, and the silence that ensued from it, much of the subsequent intellectual fate of the French Left was — we can now see — being decided. Twelve years later, Sartre ended his career with a study of Flaubert whose monumental proportions could not conceal — in their own way even advertised — the modesty of his reversion to the biographical micro-project of *The Question of Method*.

In the interim, the entire terrain — the high ground, with its bluffs and escarpments — of theoretical contest had been evacuated. For in 1962, Lévi-Strauss had published *The Savage Mind*. Hard on the heels of the *Critique of Dialectical Reason*, it contained not only an entirely alternative anthropology, in every sense of the word, but concluded with a direct attack on Sartre's historicism, in the name of the invariant properties of all human minds and the equal dignity of all human societies. In one erasive gesture, it thus levelled all the pretensions of either dialectical reason or historical diachrony as Sartre had construed them — ideas which Lévi-Strauss simply assimilated to the mythology of the 'civilized' as opposed to the 'savage' mind, with no intrinsic superiority over it. Sartre, so agile and fertile an interlocutor, so indefatigable a polemicist hitherto, made no answer.

'The ultimate goal of the human sciences is not to constitute man but to dissolve him'[3], Lévi-Strauss concluded, unloosing the slogan of the decade. When a Marxist reply finally came, in 1965, it was no repudiation, but a counter-signature of the structuralist claim. Louis Althusser's two books, *For Marx* and *Reading Capital*, rather than engaging with Lévi-Strauss's attack on history or his interpretation of humanism, endorsed and incorporated them into a Marxism that was now itself reinterpreted as a theoretical anti-humanism, for which diachrony was no more than the 'development of the forms' of synchronic knowledge itself. Sartre, Althusser confided in the pages of the weekly of the Italian Communist Party, was a false friend of historical materialism, actually more distant from it than its ostensible critic Levi-Strauss.[4] The novelty and ingenuity of the Althusserian

---

3. *The Savage Mind*, London 1966, pp. 254-255, 247 (trs. modified).
4. See his two-part intervention published under the titles 'Teoria e Metodo' and

system were, in their own right, undeniable: I have defended their legacy elsewhere.[5] They very quickly acquired a vast prestige and influence on the French Left, displacing anterior theoretical currents — represented not only by Sartre but equally by Lefebvre, Goldmann and others — virtually entirely in the formation of a younger generation of Marxists. But even at the peak of its productivity, Althusserianism was always constituted in an intimate and fatal dependence on a structuralism that both preceded it and would survive it. Lévi-Strauss had peremptorily sought to cut the Gordian knot of the relation between structure and subject by suspending the latter from any field of scientific knowledge. Rather than resisting this move, Althusser radicalized it, with a version of Marxism in which subjects were abolished altogether, save as the illusory effects of ideological structures. But in an objectivist auction of this kind, he was bound to be outbid. A year later his former pupil Foucault, proclaiming a full-throated rhetoric of the 'end of man', in turn reduced Marxism itself to an involuntary effect of an out-dated Victorian episteme, and no more than a derivative one at that.[6] The advance of structuralism, far from being deflected or halted by the new reading of Marxism, was — for all the latter's protestations of distance — accelerated by it.

The most striking evidence of the resultant pattern of hegemony was furnished by the test of the May events in France. Here, it might have seemed plausible to think, structuralism as a stance would have encountered its discomfiture at the hands of a historical dynamic it had sought to side-track or deny. What more spectacular irruption of individual and collective subjects could be imagined than the revolt of students, workers and so many others in 1968? If any species of the reigning discourses before May should have been able to respond to this signal political explosion of the class struggle, and survive in theorizing it, one would have though that the indicated candidate was

'Gli Strumenti del Marxismo', in *Rinascita*, 25 January and 1 February 1964, criticizing views expressed by Umberto Eco on main currents within contemporary culture. This text has been consistently overlooked in the standard bibliographies of Althusser's writings.

5. *Arguments within English Marxism*, London 1980.
6. *The Order of Things*, London 1970, pp. 261-262.

logically the Marxist variant developed by Althusser. For, however unadapted to the change in other ways, it did at least possess a theory of contradiction and over-determination, and therewith of the kind of 'ruptural unity'[7] which could give rise to just such a revolutionary situation in a class-divided society as had all but occurred in France. In fact, the exact opposite occurred. Althusser did attempt to adjust his theory by belatedly granting space to the role of the 'masses', who, he now conceded, 'made history', even if 'men and women' did not.[8] But since the overall direction of Althusser's enquiries was neither corrected nor developed, the introduction of the problem of the historical subject into the machinery of structural causality set out in *Reading Capital* simply resulted in incoherence. No new synthesis comparable to his earlier work appeared. The consequence was the progressive effacement and dissolution of Althusserian Marxism, as a current, by the mid-seventies.

By contrast, structuralism proper, contrary to every expectation, passed through the ordeal of May and re-emerged phoenix-like on the other side — extenuated and modulated, it is true, but by no less and no more than the equivocal prefix of a chronology: where structuralism once had been, now post-structuralism was. The exact relationship between the two, the family resemblance or common descent that unites them across the slim temporal marker, remains to be established. It may prove to be the most revealing feature of both. But few have doubted the existence of the bond between them. Indeed, two of the most central figures of the first were no less prominent in the second: Lacan, whose *Ecrits* — gathered in 1966, with much structuralist *réclame* — already anticipated much of the internal critique of structuralism developed after 1968; and Foucault, who moved without trouble or turmoil from the one constellation to the next, always abreast of the moment. Derrida himself, a purer post-structuralist thinker whose first trio of works published in 1967 prepared the positions for the general 'reversal of verdicts' after May, for all his fastidious cavils at Lévi-Strauss, could not but render homage to him as the seeker for a 'new status of discourse' in which 'everything begins with structure, configuration or relationship', yet at the same

7. See *For Marx*, London 1969, pp.99-100.
8. *Lenin and Philosophy*, London 1971, pp. 21-22.

time in the 'abandonment of all reference to a centre, to a subject, to an origin, or to an absolute *archia*.'[9]

During the seventies, then, the relegation of Marxism to the margins of Parisian culture became ever more pronounced. Sartre's *Flaubert*, when it finally appeared, had virtually the air of a posthumous work — not to the life of the author, but to the cycle of culture in which it was conceived. Althusser's writing petered out in exiguous fragments and glosses. Meanwhile, structuralism and its progeny continued to be prodigiously productive. In the twenty years since the publication of *The Savage Mind*, there have been Lévi-Strauss's anthropological tetralogy on myths; the gathering flow of Lacan's essays and seminars (twenty volumes promised) on psychoanalysis; Michel Foucault's serried studies, accompanied by procedural commentaries, on madness, medicine, imprisonment and sexuality; the protean work of Barthes on literature and the numberless deconstructions of Derrida in philosophy, not to speak of the accumulating oeuvre of Deleuze and others. Seldom can the outward signs of an intellectual victory have appeared so conclusive. Yet it still remains to ask: in what did this victory consist? In what way, and to what extent, did structuralism and post-structuralism have superior answers to the problem on which they built their fortune and illustrated their ascendancy over Marxism in France — that of the relationship of structure to subject? A teeming literature opens up here, which there can be no question of exploring with adequate nuance or detail.

I will confine myself, therefore, to the demarcation of a basic space in which structuralist and post-structuralist theories can be unified, as a series of possible moves or logical operations within a common field. None of the thinkers I have mentioned, or will cite, has made every one of these moves, just as there is no full agreement between any two of them. Yet all their major themes and claims fall within the boundaries of this shared purlieu. The first operation — I say first, because it initiated the emergence of structuralism as such — involves what we could call the *exorbitation of language*. The originating discipline from which structuralism drew virtually all of its distinctive concepts was linguistics. It was here that De Saussure developed the

9. *Writing and Difference*, London 1979, p.286.

opposition between *langue* and *parole* ('language' and 'speech'), the contrast between synchronic and diachronic orders, and the notion of the sign as a unity of signifier and signified, whose relationship to its referent was essentially arbitrary or unmotivated within any given language. The scientific advance represented by Saussure's *General Course in Linguistics* was in its own field a decisive one. The application of his concepts outside the discipline for which he forged them started, moderately enough, in literary studies with the work of Jakobson and the Prague School. Here linguistic materials were still being treated, even if by definition, as particular works of literature, they lay to the *parole* side of Saussure's division rather than to the *langue* side he had considered uniquely amenable to systematic analysis. From Jakobson, the Saussurian instrumentarium passed to Lévi-Strauss, and it was with his intrepid generalization of it to his own anthropological domain that 'structuralism' as a movement was born. 'Kinship systems,' he declared, were 'a kind of language' suited to the forms of analysis that Troubetzkoy and Jakobson had pioneered for phonology. Developing this identification, he contended that marriage rules and kinship systems were such because they formed 'a set of processes permitting the establishment, between individuals and groups, of a certain type of communication. That the mediating factor in this case should be the women of the group, who are circulated between clans, lineages or families, in place of the words of the group . . . does not at all change the fact that the essential aspect of the phenomenon is identical in both cases.'[10]

Once this equation was made, it was a short step to extend it to *all* the major structures of society, as Lévi-Strauss saw them: the economy itself was now added, under the rubric of an exchange of goods forming a symbolic system comparable to the exchange of women in kin networks and the exchange of words in language. The next major extension of the linguistic model was, of course, Lacan's reformulation of psychoanalytic theory. 'The unconscious,' he announced, 'is structured like a language.'[11] The application here was in fact more radical than this famous dictum implies. For the actual burden of Lacan's work is not that the unconscious is structured 'like' a language,

10. *Structural Anthropology*, London 1964, p.60.
11. E.g.: *The Four Fundamental Concepts of Psychoanalysis*, London 1977, p.20.

but rather that it is language as such that forms the alienating domain of the unconscious, as the Symbolic Order that institutes the unsurpassable and irreconcilable Other and therewith, at the same stroke, desire and its repression down through the chain of signifiers. After such fundamental expansions of the jurisdiction of language, there inevitably followed a host of lesser adventures and annexations: clothes, cars, cooking, and other items of fashion or consumption were subjected to diligent semiological scrutiny, derived from structural linguistics. The final step along this path was to be taken by Derrida, who — marking the post-structuralist break — rejected the notion of language as a stable system of objectification, but radicalized its pretensions as a *universal* suzerain of the modern world, with the truly imperial decree, 'there is nothing outside of the text', 'nothing before the text, no pretext that is not already a text'.[12] The Book of the World that the Renaissance, in its naïveté, took to be a metaphor, becomes the last, literal word of a philosophy that would shake all metaphysics.

It was Saussure himself, ironically, who warned against exactly the abusive analogies and extrapolations from his own domain that have been so unstoppable in the past decades. Language, he wrote, is 'a human institution of such a kind that all the other human institutions, with the exception of writing, can only deceive us as to its real essence if we trust in their analogy'.[13] Indeed, he singled out kinship and economy — precisely the two systems with whose assimilation to language Lévi-Strauss inaugurated structuralism as a general theory — as incommensurable with it. Familial institutions such as monogamy or polygamy, he noted, were improper objects for semiological analysis, because they were far from unmotivated in the same way as the sign. Economic relations were likewise unamenable to his categories because economic value was 'rooted in things and in their natural relations' — 'the value of a plot of ground, for instance, is related to its productivity'.[14] Saussure's whole effort, ignored by his

---

12. *Of Grammatology*, Baltimore 1976, p.158; *Dissemination*, Chicago 1981, p.328.

13. 'Notes Inédites de Ferdinand de Saussure', in *Cahiers Ferdinand de Saussure*, No. 12, 1954, p.60. Far the best account of the origins and tensions of Saussure's thought is to be found in Sebastiano Timpanaro, *On Materialism*, London 1976, pp. 135-158, which discusses this and similar passages.

14. Saussure, *Course in General Linguistics*, London 1960, pp.73, 80.

borrowers, was to emphasise the *singularity* of language, everything that separated it from other social practices or forms: 'We are deeply convinced,' he declared, 'that whoever sets foot on the terrain of language can be said to be bereft of all the analogies of heaven and earth.'[15] In fact, the analogies that were to be promptly discovered by Lévi-Strauss or Lacan, in their extension of linguistic categories to anthropology or psychoanalysis, give way on the smallest critical inspection. Kinship cannot be compared to language as a system of symbolic communication in which women and words are respectively 'exchanged', as Lévi-Strauss would have it, since no speaker alienates vocabulary to any interlocutor, but can freely reutilize every word 'given' as many times as is wished thereafter, whereas marriages — unlike conversations — are usually binding: wives are not recuperable by their fathers after their weddings. Still less does the terminology of 'exchange' warrant an elision to the economy: if speakers and families in most societies may be reckoned to have at least a rough equivalence of words and women between them, this is notoriously not true of goods. No economy, in other words, can be primarily defined in terms of exchange at all: production and property are always prior. Lévi-Strauss's trinitarian formula operates, in effect, to screen out all the relations of power, exploitation and inequality which inhere not only in most primitive economies, let alone our civilization of capital, but also in every familial or sexual order known to us, in which conjugality is tied to property, and femininity to subalternity. Familiar considerations of this sort hold equally good in the case of Lacan. Far from the unconscious being structured like a language, or coinciding with it, Freud's construction of it as the object of psychoanalytic enquiry precisely defines it as *in*capable of the generative grammar which, for a post-Saussurian linguistics, comprises the deep structures of language: that is, the competence to form sentences and carry out correctly the rules of their transformations. The Freudian unconscious, innocent even of negation, is a stranger to all syntax.

These local objections, conclusive as they may be for the disciplines in question, nevertheless do not in themselves convey the general reason why language is no fitting model for any other human practice.

15. 'Notes Inédites de Ferdinand de Saussure', p.64.

We can see the distance between them most clearly, perhaps, if we recollect Lévi-Strauss's argument in *The Savage Mind* that language provides an apodictic experience of a totalizing and dialectical reality anterior and exterior to the consciousness and will of any speaking subject, whose utterances on the contrary are never conscious totalizations of linguistic laws.[16] The basic presumption of structuralism has always been that this asymmetry is paradigmatic for society and history at large. But in fact the relation between *langue* and *parole* is a peculiarly aberrant compass for plotting the diverse positions of structure and subject in the world outside language. This is so for at least three basic reasons. Firstly, linguistic structures have an exceptionally low coefficient of historical mobility, among social institutions. Altering very slowly and, with few and recent exceptions, unconsciously, they are in that respect quite unlike economic, political or religious structures, whose rates of change — once the threshold of class society has been reached — have generally been incomparably faster. Secondly, however, this characteristic immobility of language as a structure is accompanied by a no less exceptional *inventivity* of the subject within it: the obverse of the rigidity of *langue* is the volatile liberty of *parole*. For utterance has no *material* constraint whatever: words are free, in the double sense of the term. They cost nothing to produce, and can be multiplied and manipulated at will, within the laws of meaning. All other major social practices are subject to the laws of natural *scarcity*: persons, goods or powers cannot be generated *ad libitum* and *ad infinitum*. Yet the very freedom of the speaking subject is curiously inconsequential: that is, its effects on the structure in return are in normal circumstances virtually nil. Even the greatest writers, whose genius has influenced whole cultures, have typically altered the language relatively little. This, of course, at once indicates the third peculiarity of the structure-subject relationship in language: namely, the subject of speech is axiomatically *individual*— 'don't speak all together' being the customary way of saying that plural speech is non-speech, that which cannot be heard. By contrast, the relevant subjects in the domain of economic, cultural, political or military structures are first and foremost *collective*: nations, classes,

16. *The Savage Mind*, p.252.

castes, groups, generations. Precisely because this is so, the agency of *these* subjects is capable of effecting profound transformations of those structures. This fundamental distinction is an insurmountable barrier to any transposition of linguistic models to historical processes of a wider sort. The opening move of structuralism, in other words, is a speculative aggrandisement of language that lacks any comparative credentials.

What are the intellectual consequences *within* structuralism of this absolutization of language? The most important immediate effect is what we can call — and this is the second modal operation within its characteristic space — the *attenuation of truth*. Saussure had distinguished within the sign the signifier and the signified — as he thought of them, the 'acoustic image' and the 'concept'. On the one hand he emphasised the arbitrary character of the sign, relative to any referent that it 'named' — in other words, the detachability of the 'concept' from its 'sound'; on the other hand, he stressed that to the extent to which language was not simply a process of nomination, each signifier acquired its semantic value only by virtue of its differential position within the structure of *langue* — in other words, the intrication of concepts in the sound-system as a whole. Linguistic value, he wrote, 'is determined concurrently along these two axes'.[17] 'A word can be exchanged for something dissimilar, an idea', and 'it can be compared with something of the same nature, another word'.[18] The result is a precarious balance between signifier and signified in his complex conception of the sign. This equilibrium was bound to be broken once langage was taken as an all-purpose model outside the domain of verbal communication itself. For the condition of its conversion into a portable paradigm was its closure into a self-sufficient system, no longer moored to any extra-linguistic reality.

Structural*ism* as a project, then, was committed from the start to the repression of the referential axis of Saussure's theory of the sign. The result could only be a gradual megalomania of the signifier. Lévi-Strauss started the escalation of its claims with the improbable thesis that language was invented by man en bloc, as a complete system

17. *Cours de Linguistique Générale (Edition Critique)*, Vol. I, ed. Rudolf Engler, Wiesbaden 1968, p.259.
18. *Course in General Linguistics*, p 115.

already in excess of the possible uses of it. 'Man from his origin disposes of an integral stock of signifiers which he is hard put to allocate to the signified given as such without thereby being known', he wrote.[19] The result was a permanent 'superabundance of the signifier, relative to the signified on which it can pose itself'. Lacan, once again, was responsible for the next rung, when he simply identified the networks of signifiers with their differential positions within *langue*, demoting the signified to the mere flux of things said as *paroles*. Where Lévi-Strauss invoked a 'floating signifier' above an implicitly stable signified, Lacan now spoke of the 'incessant sliding of the signified *under* the signifier',[20] itself taken as a metaphor of the subject; hence the effective impossibility of signifying any stable intentional meaning because of the inter-relational dynamism of the chain of signifiers themselves, one coextensive with the unconscious, that perpetually undoes the illusory identity of the ego represented by them. Thereafter, it only remained for Derrida to reject the very notion of the sign itself, as a unity-in-distinction of the signifier and the signified, by cancelling any residual autonomy of the signified altogether. Language now becomes a process in which 'every signified is also in the position of a signifier'[21] — that is, a system of floating signifiers pure and simple, with no determinable relation to any extra-linguistic referents at all.

The necessary consequence of such a contraction of language into itself is, of course, to sever any possibility of truth as a correspondence of propositions to reality. It was Foucault and Derrida who most unflinchingly assumed the ensuing logic: in doing so, they were able to reach back beyond Saussure to the philosophical legacy of the late Nietzsche, in its relentless denunciation of the illusion of truth and the fixity of meaning. For Derrida, any concept of truth is to be equated with the compulsive metaphysics of presence, with which Nietzsche broke in his — I quote — 'joyous affirmation of the play of the world and the innocence of becoming . . . without fault, without truth and

19. 'Introduction à l'Oeuvre de Marcel Mauss', in M. Mauss, ed, *Sociologie et Anthropologie*, Paris 1950, p.xlix.
20. *Ecrits*, London 1977, p.154.
21. *Positions*, Chicago 1981, p.20.

without origin'.[22] In Foucault, the stress is less on the liberation from the cognitive in the ludic than on the tyranny of the veridical itself. The will to truth, he asserts, produces its knowledge through 'a primary and perpetually reiterated falsification which poses the distinction between the true and the false'.[23] The slippage of gear towards a free-wheeling nescience, proclaimed if never entirely practised by their juniors, remains alien to the earlier generation of structuralist thinkers. Both Lévi-Strauss and Lacan, when the occasion demands it, even affect scientistic aspirations by looking forward to the mathematization of their respective disciplines. But on closer inspection, the circular logic of a self-referential language that they bring to each of their disciplines has its predictable effects. Thus Lévi-Strauss asks 'what does it matter?' if his interpretations of myths are forced or arbitrary, since they themselves can be read as no less a myth; 'it is in the last resort immaterial whether in this book the thought processes of the South American Indians take shape through the medium of my thought, or whether mine takes place through theirs'.[24] Here it is error that is excluded from the outset, in the self-exhibiting identity of the human mind. Quite consistently, Lévi-Strauss exalts Wagner in the same pages as the true 'originator of the structural analysis of myths', who conducted his investigations in the superior medium of *music* — higher because wholly interior to itself, the art which is in principle beyond meaning or representation. The solution is similar in Lacan, who retains a vestigial concept of the Real beyond the Symbolic, but only as the 'impossible' which cannot be signified — a realm of the ineffable that, he stresses, has nothing in common with mere 'reality' as the 'ready-to-wear of fantasy'. Conversely, Lacan also earned Derrida's reproaches by preserving the notion of truth; but by truth he means the capacity of the subject to articulate desire, rather than attain knowledge. This expressive redefinition of truth eventually rejoins Lévi-Strauss. For literal accuracy has no pertinence to the 'full word' of the psychoanalytic subject, who *cannot but* speak 'truly' — i.e. symptomatically — no matter what he

22. *Writing and Difference*, p.292.
23. *Language, Counter-Memory, Practice*, Ithaca 1977, p.203: here too the express source is Nietzsche.
24. *The Raw and the Cooked*, London 1969, pp.13, 15.

or she says.[25] Here again, without untruth truth ceases to be such — as Foucault rightly saw. The *distinction* between the true and the false is the ineliminable premise of any rational knowledge. Its central site is evidence. It is no accident that the latter should be so generally disdained within the space of structuralism. Lévi-Strauss's fleeting field-work and fictive map of kinship systems; Lacan's ten-minute psychoanalytic sessions; Foucault's credulity in the Ship of Fools and fable of the Great Confinement[26] — all are not so much personal limitations or lapses of the practitioners concerned, as normal and natural licences in a play of signification beyond truth and falsehood.

The attack on representation inherent in the notion of an autotelic language has its predictable incidence on the status of causality in the space of structuralism. With this we reach the third major move describable within it, or what can be called *the randomization of history*. For once the linguistic model becomes a general paradigm in the human sciences, the notion of ascertainable cause starts to undergo a critical weakening. The reason lies in the very nature of the relationship between *langue* and *parole* within structural linguistics. The supremacy of *langue* as a system is the cornerstone of the Saussurian legacy: *parole* is the subsequent activation of certain of its resources by the speaking subject. But the priority of one over the other is of a peculiar sort: it is both unconditional and indeterminant. That is to say, an individual speech-act can only execute certain general linguistic laws, if it is to be communication at all. But at the same time, the *laws* can never explain the *act*. An unbridgeable gulf exists between the general rules of syntax and the utterance of particular sentences — whose shape or occasion can never be deduced from the sum of grammar, vocabulary or phonetics. Language as a system furnishes the formal *conditions of possibility* of speech, but has no purchase on its actual *causes*. For Saussure, the pattern of words spoken — the unravelling reel of *parole* — necessarily fell outside the domain of linguistic science altogether:

25. *Ecrits*, Paris 1966, pp.649, 409; the first words of *Télévision*, Paris 1973, read: 'Je dis toujours la vérité', p.9.

26. For the latter, see H.C. Erik Middelfort, 'Madness and Civilization in Early Modern Europe: A Reappraisal of Michel Foucault', in Barbara Malament, ed, *After the Reformation: Essays in Honor of J.H. Hexter*, Philadelphia 1980, pp.247-265 — a critique all the more damaging for the author's *pro-forma* adherence to the conventional respects paid to Foucault.

it related to a more general history and required other principles of enquiry. The extrapolation of the linguistic model by post-Saussurian structuralism, however, typically proceeded to a tacit conflation of the two types of intelligibility. Conditions of possibility were systematically presented 'as if' they were causes. The two most extended examples of this tendential confusion were to be Lévi-Strauss's studies of mythologies in primitve societies and Foucault's attempts to construct an archaeology of knowledge in civilized ones.

In each case, a massive analytic machinery is mounted, whose essential goal is to demonstrate the *identity* of the field in question — the invariant function of totems or structure of myths, the unity of epistemes or the rigidity of discursive formations. Once constructed, however, these leave no epistemological passage to the *diversity* of specific myths or enunciations, still less to the *development* from one to another. The result is that instead of genuine explanation, structuralist analysis constantly tends to tilt towards classification: 'adjacency' as Edward Said has remarked, eclipses 'sequentiality'.[27] A failure to distinguish these two intellectual operations is the hall-mark of Lévi-Strauss's theorization of *The Savage Mind*, which concludes with the claim that there is no essential difference between the 'concrete logic' of primitive societies — that is, their taxonomies of the natural world — and the 'abstract logic' of mathematized science in civilized societies:[28] both are expressions of the same universal propensities of the human mind. The explanatory power of modern science is levelled to the classificatory magic of totemism, in a procedure which in turn underwrites the basic démarche of Lévi-Strauss himself. This is not to say that no explanations at all can be found in structuralist writing: but where they occur, they are curiously marginal or fragile, unable to focus or sustain the burden of the overall descriptions in which they pass by. Against the enormous proliferation of Lévi-Strauss's meditations on Amerindian myths, the sparse schema of their occasional reduction — to the single function of masking or mediating real contradictions, arising from the duality of Nature and Culture, in the domain of the imaginary — has as little weight as originality. Similarly, Foucault's later work on the 19th-century prison systems includes the

27. *Beginnings*, Baltimore 1978, p.302.
28. *The Savage Mind*, p.269.

50

thesis that their real function was not to suppress but to generate a criminal underclass that served to justify global policing of the population as a whole, in the 'carceral continuum' of the contemporary social order in which schools, hospitals, factories or regiments all reveal the same organizing principle. Those who police them remain anonymous. Here it is less the modesty than the melodrama of the hypothesis that make of it a siding in the work as a whole, whose effect depends on its density of description rather than force of explanation. Causality, even when granted admission, never acquires cogent centrality on the terrain of structuralist analysis.

What then becomes of history proper? A total initial determinism paradoxically ends in the reinstatement of an absolute final contingency, in mimicry of the duality of *langue* and *parole* itself. The most striking example of this irony is Derrida's work, which amalgamates the entire history of Western philosophy into a single homogeneous metaphysics, defined by the ubiquitous identity of its quest for 'presence', while on the other hand any individual sentence or paragraph within the spokesmen of that metaphysic is seamed and undermined by the irreducible heterogeneity of *différance*. Writing is thus at once implacable and undecidable, inescapably the same in its general structure and inexplicably differing and deferring in its particular textualizations. The same antinomy punctually recurs in the thought of Lévi-Strauss and Foucault. Lévi-Strauss ends *From Honey to Ashes* by disavowing any 'refusal of history'; but the place he accords it is a purely aleatory one. 'Structural analysis,' he writes, concedes to history 'that which by right belongs to irreducible contigency', it makes its bow to 'the power and inanity of the event'.[29] The profoundest *historical* transformations — the Neolithic or Industrial Revolutions — can thus be theorized by Lévi-Strauss in terms of a multiple roulette game, where the winning combination that makes possible these upheavals is achieved by a coalition of players at several wheels, rather than an individual — that is, by a group of societies rather than a single one.[30] Diachronic development, in other words, is reduced to the chance outcome of a synchronic combinatory. Foucault, likewise unable to explain the sudden mutations between the successive

29. *From Honey to Ashes*, London 1973, p.475 (trs. modified).
30. *Race and History*, Paris 1952, pp.37-39.

epistemes of his early work, each of which are treated as homogeneous unities, later resorted to increasing celebration of the role of *chance* as the governor of events, which — he argued in *The Order of Discourse* — should be seen no longer in terms of cause and effect, but of the serial and the unpredictable. In practice, Foucault's subsequent work has converted these methodological prescriptions into an ontology — a panurgic will to power pulsing through all social and psychic structures of whatever sort. Their common derivation from Nietzsche indicates the linkage between chance and power, so interpreted, in Foucault's thought. Once hypostatized as a new First Principle, Zarathustra-style, power loses any historical determination: there are no longer specific holders of power, nor any specific goals which its exercise serves. As sheer *will*, its exercise is its own satisfaction. But since such will is all-pervasive, it must generate its own contrary. 'Where there is power, there is resistance' — but this resistance is, it too, a counter-power.[31] In the frontierless flux of conation conjured up by the later Foucault, causality as an intelligible necessity of social relationships or historical events disappears: the mutual contention is unconditioned, and its outcome can only be contingent. Power *is* the inanity of the event, in this version. Power relationships are 'reversible' — as Foucault puts it — in the same sense and for the same theoretical reasons as textual significations are 'undecidable' for Derrida. Said's oxymoron sums up what can properly be called the structuralist philosophy of history — 'legislated accident'.[32]

It may now be easier to see why structuralism should have engendered post-structuralism with such facility and congruity. For the transit from one to the other represents the final move logically available within the space we have been delimiting. This could be termed the *capsizal of structures* themselves. Why should the apparently ascetic objectivism of the mid sixties — the moment, shall we say, of *The Order of Things* — have so often issued into the saturnalian subjectivism of the mid seventies — the moment of *Anti-Œdipus* —

---

31. 'There are no relations of power without resistances', for 'resistance to power' is 'the compatriot of power': *Power/Knowledge*, Brighton 1980, p.142.

32. *Beginnings*, p.311; or, in Nietzsche's phrase exalted by Foucault, 'the iron hand of necessity shaking the dice-box of chance' — see *Language, Counter-Memory, Practice*, p.155.

without major rupture of continuity among men and ideas? The answer lies in the problem posed for any thoroughgoing structuralism by its cognitive starting point. For if structures alone obtain in a world beyond all subjects, what secures their objectivity? High structuralism was never more strident than in its annunciation of the end of man. Foucault struck the characteristically prophetic note when he declared in 1966: 'Man is in the process of perishing as the being of language continues to shine ever more brightly upon our horizon.'[33] But who is the 'we' to perceive or possess such a horizon? In the hollow of the pronoun lies the aporia of the programme. Lévi-Strauss opted for the most consistent solution to it. While echoing — even cosmically amplifying — Foucault in his sightings of 'the twilight of man', he postulated a basic isomorphism between nature and mind, reflected equally in myths and the structural analysis of them. Mind repeats nature in myths because it is itself nature, and the structural method repeats the operations of myths that it studies; or, in Lévi-Strauss's words, 'Myths signify the mind which evolves them by making use of the world of which it is itself a part'.[34] Amidst a plethora of denunciations of philosophy, what reappears in *Mythologiques* is thus one of the oldest figures of classical idealism — the identical subject-object.

But the identity is, of course, also a figment: for what Lévi-Strauss cannot explain is the emergence of his own discipline itself. How do the unconscious mental structures of the primitive become the conscious discoveries of the anthropologist? The discrepancy between the two fatally retables the question of what guarantees that these *are* discoveries, rather than arbitrary fancies. In the cult of music with which his tetralogy begins and ends, lies the abandonment of any answer: 'the supreme mystery of the science of man', music holds for Lévi-Strauss 'the key to the progress'[35] of all other branches. The Wagnerian rapture here was no mere personal idiosyncrasy. *The Birth of Tragedy*, apotheosis of Wagner and theorization of music as the parent of language, is also the source-work of the theme of an original Dionysiac frenzy, as the Other of all Apollonian order, that has always underlain Foucault's work. For him, too, the difficulty was to account

33. *The Order of Things*, p.386.
34. *The Raw and the Cooked*, p.341.
35. *The Raw and the Cooked*, p.18.

for the capacity of the archaeologist to uncover the archives of knowledge, or reconstruct the temporal differences between them, given the closure — 'very tight-knit, very coherent'[36] — of the modern episteme itself. What then barred the way to a complete relativism? Unconfessable as such, the continuity of Foucault's research in fact rested from the outset on the appeal to an untamed primal experience anterior to all the successive orders of Western Reason, and subversive of them, in whose eyes their common nature as repressive structures stands revealed. 'Throughout the history of the West *the necessity of madness,*' he wrote in his first important work, 'is linked to *the possibility of history.*'[37] Madness as pure alterity — the sound which must be stilled for the speech of rational sociality to develop as its voluble negation — recedes in the later Foucault, as the concept of repression itself becomes suspect as another ruse of Reason. But the tacit principle of the originary Other persists, in new guises. In his most recent work it is the innocence of 'the body and its pleasures',[38] in their unity, as opposed to mere socially confected and divided 'sexuality', which performs the same function — an unnameable indictment.

With Derrida, the self-cancellation of structuralism latent in the recourse to music or madness in Lévi-Strauss or Foucault is consummated. With no commitment to exploration of social realities at all, Derrida had little compunction in undoing the constructions of these two, convicting them both of a 'nostalgia of origins' — Rousseauesque or pre-Socratic, respectively — and asking what right either had to assume, on their own premises, the validity of their discourses. 'If the mythological is mythomorphic, are all discourses on myths equivalent?', he enquired on the one hand. On the other hand, how could a 'history of madness', he asked, 'as it carries itself and breathes before being caught and paralysed in the nets of classical reason', be written 'from within the very language of classical reason itself, utilizing the concepts that were the historical instruments of the

---

36. *The Order of Things*, p.384, where Foucault opts for the artless solution that the 'logic' of the modern episteme leads to its own supersession, in a simple evolutionism.

37. *Folie et Déraison: Histoire de la Folie à l'Age Classique*, Paris 1961, p.vi: author's italics.

38. *The History of Sexuality*, London 1978, p.157.

capture of madness'?[39] The common vice of all previous intellectual traditions was to 'neutralize or reduce' the 'stucturality of structure' by 'giving it a centre or referring it to a point of presence, a fixed origin' that itself 'escaped structurality', in such a way as to limit 'the *play* of structure'.[40] What Derrida had seen, acutely, was that the supposition of any stable structure had always depended on the silent postulation of a centre that was not entirely 'subject' to it: in other words, of a *subject* distinct *from* it. His decisive move was to liquidate the last vestige of such autonomy. The result, however, was not to achieve a higher-order, now entirely purified structure, but the very contrary: the effect was a radically *destructuring* one. For once structures were freed from any subject at all, delivered over totally to their own play, they would lose what *defines* them as structures — that is, any objective coordinates of organization at all. Structurality, for Derrida, is little more than a ceremonious gesture to the prestige of his immediate predecessors: its play now knows no boundaries of any sort — it is 'absolute chance', 'genetic indetermination', 'the seminal adventure of the trace'.[41] Structure therewith capsizes into its antithesis, and post-structuralism proper is born, or what can be defined as a subjectivism without a subject.

The lesson is that structure and subject have in this sense always been *interdependent* as categories. A wholesale attack on the latter was bound to subvert the former in due course as well. The terminus of the operation could only be a finally unbridled subjectivity. Adorno had foreseen this development, often remarking that any theory which sought completely to deny the illusory power of the subject would tend to reinstate that illusion even more than one which overestimated the power of the subject.[42] The structuralist thinker who resisted this

39. *Writing and Difference*, pp. 287 and 34.
40. *Writing and Difference*, pp. 278-279.
41. *Writing and Difference*, p.292.
42. 'The objectivity of truth really demands the subject. Once cut off from the subject, it becomes the victim of sheer subjectivity': *Against Epistemology*, Oxford 1982, p 72. The encapsulation above is the happy formula of Gillian Rose, in *The Melancholy Science — An Introduction to the Thought of Theodor W. Adorno*, London 1978, p.128. Note, however, that in his reflections on the dialectic of the two, Adorno insisted that 'the question of the share of each is not to be settled generally and invariably': *Against Epistemology*, p 156.

movement more than any other was Lacan, precisely because he had started out with a firmer commitment to the subject itself — both from his psychoanalytic profession, where the category could not so lightly be disposed of, and because of his prior philosophical formation, essentially Hegelian rather than Nietzschean or Heideggerian. But his conception of the subject, which abrogated the role of the ego and rescinded the reality principle, as Freud had posited them, to give plenipotentiary powers to a — dematerialized — id alone, cleared the way for its own supersession. Deleuze and Guattari could trump it by turning on the Law of the Symbolic itself, as a removable repression, in the name of the Imaginary and its schizophrenic objects. The disintegrated desiring machines of *Anti-Œdipus*, bereft of unity or identity, are the final dénouement of the capsizal of psychic structures themselves into a subjectivity pulverized beyond measure or order.

If this, then, has been the approximate curve of the trajectory from structuralism to post-structuralism, our initial question answers itself. The unresolved difficulties and deadlocks within Marxist theory, which structuralism promised to transcend, were never negotiated in detail within this rival space. The adoption of the language model as the 'key to all mythologies', far from clarifying or decoding the relations between structure and subject, led from a rhetorical absolutism of the first to a fragmented fetishism of the second, without ever advancing a theory of their *relations*. Such a theory, historically determinate and sectorally differentiated, could only be developed in a dialectical respect for their interdependence.

3
Nature and History

The puzzle which I discussed yesterday was the reason for the retreat of Latin Marxism, at a time of general advance of Marxist culture elsewhere in the Western world. The hypothesis which seemed initially the most attractive — its intellectual defeat at the hands of a superior alternative, the structuralist culture that won dominance in Paris from the mid-sixties onwards — proved on closer scrutiny of the structuralist space itself to be an implausible one. The formal battle-field between the two, the problem of the relations between structure and subject, was never occupied in sufficient depth by structuralism to present any real challenge to a historical materialism confident of itself. An intrinsic explanation, from within the logic of the ideas of the time, meets a *fin de non recevoir* here, referring us back to the extrinsic history of politics and society at large. If we consider this plane of our problem, we can immediately notice something that tends to confirm the conclusion that, for all the polemical *atmosphere* of the period, little direct and genuine engagement occurred between the two antagonists. This is the striking political heteronomy of structuralism as a phenomenon. At no point, from the early sixties to the early eighties, have it or its sequels defended an independent social viewpoint of their own. Rather, what has distinguished structuralism and post-structuralism is the extraordinary *lability* of the political connotations they have successively assumed. This external history is essentially one of passive adaptation to the prevailing fashions and moods of the time.

Initially most of the leading structuralist thinkers paid formal homage to Marxism, at a time when it still enjoyed a post-Liberation ascendancy in France. Lévi-Strauss declared his researches to be no more than superstructural studies, complementary to the Marxist account of 'the undoubted primacy of infrastructures'.[1] Foucault started out by speaking well of Pavlov and Soviet psychiatry. Barthes's two major poles of contemporary reference were Brecht and Sartre. Lacan's close collaborator Pontalis was a member of *Les Temps Modernes* throughout the period of the latter's rapprochement with the French Communist Party. By the mid sixties, this had already altered in the consolidated climate of High Gaullism. Barthes's bland semiology of fashion was by now a far cry from his caustic *Mythologies*. Foucault's political credo veered towards a technocratic functionalism, even claiming that 'an optimal functioning of society can be defined in an internal manner, without it being possible to say "for whom" it is better that things should be thus'.[2] Then, after the May events, as structuralism swung round into post-structuralism, Foucault just as easily found his place in the neo-anarchist current dominant in much of the French Left, becoming a major spokesman of libertarian leftism, in company with Deleuze and Lyotard, while Derrida's collaborators at *Tel Quel* championed Maoism. Today, Lévi-Strauss speaks of Marxism as a totalitarian threat even to the animal kingdom; Foucault applauds the literature of gulagism; Sollers and Kristeva of *Tel Quel* have rediscovered the virtues of Christianity and capitalism. Conservative or collusive as these positions may be, they have little actual edge or weight. It is less their iniquity than their fatuity that is striking. Reflections of a political conjuncture in an essentially unpolitical thought, they can alter again when the conjuncture alters. They tell us something general about French history in the past decades, little that is specific about the ideas of structuralism itself.

This can perhaps be seen especially clearly if we look across the Rhine. In discussing the changing map of Marxism earlier, I made no mention of Germany, where a much greater stability has obtained than in either the Latin or Anglophone zones. Historical materialism has always possessed a peculiar position in the *Bundesrepublik*. On the

1. *The Savage Mind*, p.130.
2. See his declarations in Paolo Caruso, *Conversazioni con Lévi-Strauss, Foucault, Lacan*, Milan 1969, p.126; for characteristically ingenuous comments on causality, note pp.105-106. The best discussion of Foucault's political pronouncements can be found in Peter Dews's astringent essay 'The *Nouvelle Philosophie* and Foucault', *Economy and Society*, vol. 8, No 2, May 1979, pp. 125-176.

one hand, Germanic Marxism has had the longest and richest tradition in Europe — benefitting, as it did, not only from the contributions of German nationals themselves, but from the much wider zone of influence and attraction enjoyed by German-speaking culture in Central and Eastern Europe, that included Austria, Switzerland, Bohemia, Hungary and Poland. Luxemburg, Kautsky, Bauer and Lukács all came from these borderlands. It was here too that Freud's discoveries, of course, made their first wider intellectual impact. The Weimar period saw the rise of the Institute for Social Research in Frankfurt and the emergence of the theatre of Piscator and Brecht, amidst a general culture of the Left of great brilliance and vitality, whose social backcloth was the strongest labour movement in the West, with the largest and most dynamic Communist Party. After exile and the war, most of the Frankfurt School could come back to West Germany, as Brecht did to East Germany, and develop its work in a creative continuity with pre-war themes and debates that was unique in Europe. On the other hand, by the end of the Allied Occupation, German Communism had been crushed in the West and the labour movement firmly subordinated to capitalism: by the mid-fifties, the Social-Democratic Party had formally abandoned any allegiance to Marxism, and the Communist Party was proscribed. The politics of Adenauer's Germany rivalled those of Eisenhower's America in their stifling conformity and reaction.

Frankfurt Marxism, formed in another epoch and tempered in adversity abroad, as a whole did not bend to the new Restoration of the German 'Miracle'. But its distance from directly political discourse or engagement, already great before the war, became well-nigh absolute. Yet within the universities, its influence nurtured the emergence of a very large, increasingly militant layer of students whose rebellion in 1968 revealed that Marxism had become disseminated and diversified anew in a numerous younger generation of socialist intellectuals. By then Horkheimer was in his Swiss dotage. Adorno, profoundly taken aback by the eruption of his own pupils, died a year later. It was left to Habermas, the major thinker to emerge from the post-war levy of the Frankfurt tradition, to confront the student movement as a force. Bruised by direct attacks on himself and his colleagues, he denounced the SDS as coercive and irrationalist, and withdrew from the university. Already a prolific writer in the sixties, his oeuvre steadily developed and expanded over the next decade, coming to represent the most comprehensive and ambitious theoretical project of the contemporary German scene.

The fruition of this work makes it clear that the absence of any reference to Habermas in *Considerations on Western Marxism* was, in fact, a major error of appreciation. There were two reasons for that omission. One was Habermas's own response to the upheavals of the late sixties, expressed in impromptu formulations that appeared to disqualify him as a political thinker of any weight. The second, and more important, was the hybrid character of his philosophical work as such, revealing as it did pervasive importations from American pragmatism and action theory into a Frankfurt heritage in certain respects more directly reworked through Hegel, albeit of the Jena period, than ever before. That seemed to render questionable its inclusion within the framework of even an ecumenically understood Marxism.[3] Such motivations were not without plausibility. In an attractive recent interview, Habermas himself has alluded to the grounds for them, at once retracting his psychologistic comments on the student movement as ill-judged, and remarking how difficult he too found it to know whether his work should or should not be regarded as Marxist. (Its initial description as such, with the publication of *Strukturwandel der Öffentlichkeit* in the early sixties, came to him as a surprise, he recounts.) Yet the same interview, while freely discussing the continuing ambiguities of his intellectual position, expresses a modest and straightforward desire for affiliation to historical materialism today, sufficient in itself to quash conventional earlier judgements of his evolution.[4] Behind such declarations, in fact, now stands a commanding body of work seeking, in Habermas's own terms, to

3. Another case of a similar type was posed by the thought of Ernst Bloch — no less unjustly omitted from my brief survey, because of its constant adjacency to forms of religious *Naturphilosophie*. For an excellent study of Bloch's difficult work, written in a spirit of critical sympathy that brings out the originality of his contribution to the Western Marxist canon, see now Wayne Hudson, *The Marxist Philosophy of Ernst Bloch*, London 1982.

4. 'Today I value being considered a Marxist': 'Interview with Jürgen Habermas', *New German Critique*, No. 18, Fall 1979, p.33. The whole tenor of this text, the best biographical account of Habermas's development, can be profitably compared with Althusser's asseverations of the same period: see note 26, p.30 above.

'reconstruct' historical materialism in keeping with the critical transformation of the Frankfurt tradition he has effected. The architectural
scale and sweep of the theoretical edifice that has resulted — syn-
thesizing epistemological, sociological, psychological, political, cultural and ethical enquiries in a single programme of research — has no
real parallel in contemporary philosophy, of whatever inspiration. A
proper sense of the distinction of this achievement should be the
starting-point for any evaluation of Habermas's work. The ideas that
have interlocked to form his philosophical system need, however, to
be situated with some comparative calipers.

For if we look at the characteristic coordinates of Habermas's
thought, the first thing that must strike any attentive observer is how
close many of them are to those of French structuralism. The same
premises and preoccupations recur again and again, albeit each time
from different sources and with different conclusions. The starting
point of Habermas's distinctive position, as it were on the border-line
between Marxism and non-Marxism, was his argument that Marx
erred in giving a fundamental primacy to material production in his
definition of humanity as a species and in his conception of history as
an evolution of societal forms. 'Social interaction', Habermas main-
tained, was an equally irreducible dimension of human practice. Such
interaction was always symbolically mediated, constituting the specific
domain of communicative activity — as opposed to the instrumental
activity of material production. Where production was aimed at increasing control over external nature, interaction generated those
norms that adapted inner nature — human needs and dispositions —
to social life. There was no necessary correspondence between the
two: economic or scientific progress did not necessarily assure cultural
or political liberation. The 'dialectic of moral life', as he called it, had
its own autonomy.

This original base-line of the Habermasian programme — a doctrine
of 'separate but equal' types of human activity — then underwent a
series of crucial shifts as his work developed. Three conceptual
slippages, in particular, occurred. First the notion of social interaction — vague enough in all conscience, but generically denoting the
realm of cultural and political forms in their widest sense, as opposed
to the economy — tended increasingly to give way to that of com-

munication, as if the two were simply equivalent, the latter being more precise. But, of course, there are many forms of social interaction that are not, except in a purely abusive or metaphoric sense, communication: war, one of the most salient practices in human history, is the most obvious example, while the associated labour of material production is itself social interaction of the most basic kind. Next, however, communication came to be increasingly identified with language, as if these two were also interchangeable — despite the familiar multiplicity of non-linguistic types of communication, from the gestural to the plastic or musical. Once this slide from communication to language had occurred, the next step was to subsume production itself under a common rubric derived *from* communication. This was achieved with the extension of the notion of 'learning processes' from cultural to economic systems, as the basic evolutionary category explaining the development from one level of the forces of production to another, in the course of human history. The third stage was then to assert the outright *primacy* of the communicative over the productive functions in the definition of humanity and the development of history alike: that is, in Habermas's terms, of 'language' over 'labour'. Already at the time of *Knowledge and Human Interests* Habermas declared — striking a Vichian note — 'what raises us out of nature is the only thing whose nature we can know: *language*'.[5] By the time of his *Reconstruction of Historical Materialism* of the mid-seventies, the claim is given an ontogenetic foundation. Whereas hominids practised labour with tools, revealing it as a pre-human activity, *homo sapiens* as a species was characterized by the innovation of language and the family that it alone could institute. Moreover, this privilege of communication over production is not simply constitutive of what it meant to become fully 'human'; it continues to operate as the dominant principle of historical change thereafter. For in the long development of the two sets of learning-processes between palaeolithic and capitalist societies, it is moral regulations rather than economic forces that have determined major transformations — they, indeed, which have prompted or permitted the successive reorderings of economic relationships associated with the evolution of civilization, rather than

5. *Knowledge and Human Interests*, London 1972, p.314.

vice versa. As Habermas writes: 'The development of these normative structures is the pace-maker of social evolution, for new organizational principles of social organization mean new forms of social integration; and the latter, in turn, make it possible to implement available productive forces, or to generate new ones, as well as making possible a heightening of social complexity.'[6]

This position would seem to conflict directly with the suggestion, pervasive in Habermas's early work, that normative development, 'the dialectics of the moral life', far from setting the pace of economic progress, has tended to lag disastrously behind it; or, as he explained in terms very close to the classical concepts of the Frankfurt School, that 'liberation from hunger and misery does not necessarily converge with liberation from servitude and degradation, for there is no automatic developmental relation between labour and interaction'.[7] Habermas resolves the difficulty by resorting to the notion of a 'developmental logic' of the human mind, that is, a structure at once crescent and invariant, borrowed from Piaget's genetic psychology and projected from the individual to the societal plane. This logic specifies in advance the gamut of possible normative patterns in social evolution, while at the same time grading them along a spectrum of increasing degrees of maturity. All civilizational forms, in this sense, are embryonically contained in the acquisition of language itself: 'Cognitive and interactive developments,' Habermas writes, 'no doubt merely exhaust the logical range of possible structural formations that already emerged with the natural-historical innovation of linguistically established intersubjectivity at the threshhold of the socio-cultural form of life.'[8] What, then, is the relation between the formal 'logical range' and the actual 'historical record' of successive societies?

For Habermas, the answer is that the sequence of concrete social formations in history is essentially contingent. His 'theory of social evolution' explains the 'developmental logics [that] betoken the independence — and to this extent the internal history — of the mind',[9]

6. *Communication and the Evolution of Society*, London 1979, p.120.
7. *Theory and Practice*, London 1974, p.169.
8. *Zur Rekonstruktion des historischen Materialismus*, Frankfurt 1976, p.38. This sentence is omitted in the English translation of the same essay in *Communication and the Evolution of Society*.
9. *Communication and the Evolution of Society*, p.123. Trs. modified.

whereas historiographic *narrative* studies the fortuitous circumstances and ways in which these persistent mental structures, of different levels of maturity, find their social expression. There is an impassable gulf fixed between the two. 'Evolution-theoretic explanations,' he insists, 'not only do not *need* to be further transformed into a narrative; they *cannot* be brought into narrative form.'[10] There is thus no guarantee that the contemporary social order corresponds to the highest stage of moral development inscribed in the processional logic of the mind. To that extent, Habermas retains the critical emphasis of his original distinction between the 'makeability' of a cumulative economic progress, and the 'maturity' of the socio-ethical subjects capable — or rather incapable — of assuring responsible control of it. Yet once the process of communicative learning is accorded causal primacy in historical development, and is itself founded on an inherent potential for moral growth in every human mind, there is a built-in tendency for the theory to swing towards a benign providentialism. This is the sense of Habermas's 'universal pragmatics'. Language here becomes, not merely the hallmark of humanity as such, but the promissory note of democracy — itself conceived as essentially the communication necessary to arrive at a consensual truth. A dual euphoric elision sets in. Language as such is identified with an aspiration to the good life. 'Our first sentence,' Habermas maintains, 'expresses unequivocally the intention of universal and unconstrained consensus.'[11] That consensus can always in principle be arrived at by subjects of good will, in an 'ideal speech situation'. It is this pact of agreement that establishes what is truth — and 'the truth of statements is linked in the last analysis to the intention of the good life'[12]: a life itself 'anticipated' in every act of speech, even where deceit or domination are at work, in so far as these themselves only take effect by reason of the common presumption of truth from which

10. *Zur Rekonstruktion des historischen Materialismus*, pp.244-245. 'To the functions of historical *research* for a theory of social evolution there correspond no tasks that a theory of evolution could take over for historical *writing*.' The examples Habermas gives are of the transition to archaic civilizations, with the emergence of the State, and the transition to 'modernity', with the differentiation out of a market society and the complementary emergence of a fiscal State.

11. *Knowledge and Human Interests*, p.314.

12. *Ibid.*, p.314.

they deviate. Communicative ethics are thus grounded on 'the fundamental norms of rational speech'. Psychoanalysis becomes, in this reconstruction, a theory of the 'deformation of ordinary language inter-subjectivity', whose aim is to restore to the individual the capacity for undistorted linguistic communication. At the level of the collectivity, likewise, democracy can be defined as the institutionalization of conditions for the practice of ideal — that is, domination-free — speech. It is a 'self-controlled learning process'.[13]

The similarity of the Habermasian universe and that of French structuralism and its sequels is, as can be seen, a close yet curious one. For everything that appears doubtful, dark or damned in the latter emerges translucent and redeemed in the light of the former. Both enterprises have represented sustained attempts to erect language into the final architect and arbiter of all sociability. Habermas has, if anything, articulated the underlying premise of his own ambition more clearly than any of his Parisian contemporaries, arguing — as his most authoritative commentator puts it — that 'since speech is the distinctive and pervasive medium of life at the human level, the theory of communication is the foundational study of the human sciences: it discloses the universal infrastructure of socio-cultural life'.[14] In the slide from 'medium' to 'foundation' here lies the whole confusion of the general language paradigm. But where, we might say, structuralism and post-structuralism developed a kind of diabolism of language, Habermas has unruffledly produced an angelism. In France when, as Derrida put it, 'language invaded the universal problematic'[15] — the verb, as always in his writing, is significant — it strafed meaning, over-ran truth, outflanked ethics and politics, and wiped out history. In Germany, on the contrary, in Habermas's work language restores order to history, supplies the salve of consensus to society, assures the foundations of morality, anneals the elements of democracy, and is congenitally disposed against straying from the truth. Yet for all these contrasts of conclusion and pathos, the common preoccupations and assumptions are unmistakeable.

13. *Communication and the Evolution of Society*, p.186.
14. Thomas McCarthy, *The Critical Theory of Jürgen Habermas*, Boston 1978, p.282. Habermas has rightly paid tribute to the exceptional quality of McCarthy's work as a survey of his thought.
15. *Writing and Difference*, p.280.

Typically, Habermas has sought to give a positive or rational solution to questions structuralism was content to leave negatively unresolved, or celebrated as irresoluble: but without abandoning a shared terrain. Thus Lévi-Strauss's theory of universal mental structures could provide no explanation of societal development: Habermas tries to close the gap between the two with the notion of a 'developmental logic' of these structures, generating its own combinatory. But in doing so, he ends up with exactly the same irreducible dichotomy as Foucault or Lévi-Strauss between necessity and contingency, spiritual structures and chance-governed historical processes. Discourse possesses equally thaumaturgical powers in the two opposing sets of work; but whereas, in Foucault, it signifies the exclusion of unregulable statement or determinable truth, for the registration of the servitude of the archive, it represents in Habermas the highest reach of communicative competence, the realm where ideal speech might virtually be realized, and with it the conditions of liberty as such. Lacan sees the specificity of human speech, as opposed to animal codes, in the ability to lie, while Habermas reduces all lying to a mere parasitism on the truth that it would vainly betray, in the act of speech that must betoken a promise of the true to be understood at all. Yet although Habermas insists on not only the possibility but the inevitability of truth, he is no less vehement than his Parisian opposites in condemning any correspondence theory of it as an impossible attempt 'to break out of the domain of language';[16] his own definition of it as no more than rational consensus is itself a variant of pragmatic subjectivism, separated from the abyss of Parisian relativism by no more than the tenuous safety-rail of a hypothetical 'ideal speech situation', whose counter-factuality he himself concedes. Similarly, for Lacan psychoanalysis seeks to restore to the patient the 'full word' of the unconscious, which precisely is *not* the empty accuracy of ordinary egoic language and its fixations; whereas Habermas views psychoanalysis as a therapy whose goal is to repair the subject's capacity for the 'ordinary language of intersubjectivity', with a much more traditional estimate of the positive instance of the ego, closer to that of Freud. In either case, however, a

16. 'Within which alone the claims of speech-acts to validity can be settled': 'Wahrheitstheorien', in Helmut Fahrenbach, ed., *Wirklichkeit und Reflexion: Walter Schulz zum 60. Geburtstag*, Pfullingen 1973, p.216.

dematerialization of Freud's theory has occurred, in which instinctual drives are alternatively effaced or resolved into linguistic mechanisms.

When all this has been said, it remains true that the difference between Habermas's philosophy of language and history and that of his structuralist and post-structuralist counterparts is no mere redundant one. I have spoken of the curious innocence of Habermas's vision: but this also comports a kind of integrity and dignity of thought generally foreign to the French exemplars of the language model. Habermas's very style — frequently (not always) drab, awkward, laborious — bespeaks its own contrast with the excitable *coloraturas* of the Parisian masters. Behind it lies, no *fin-de-siècle* Wagnerian overtones, but the earnest ideals and serious optimism of the German Enlightenment. *Bildung* is the real leitmotif unifying Habermas's characteristic range of interests and arguments. It leads to an essentially pedagogic view of politics, the forum become a classroom as its struggles and confrontations are transmuted into processes of learning. But for all the limitations of this optic, painfully obvious in a classical Marxist perspective, it does not actually exclude politics as such. Unlike his opposite numbers in France, Habermas has attempted a direct structural analysis of the immanent tendencies of contemporary capitalism and of the possibility of system-changing crises arising from them — in keeping with the traditional project of historical materialism. His notion of a crisis of moral 'legitimation' undermining social integration — a crisis paradoxically generated by the very success of state-directed regulation of the cycle of economic accumulation — conforms in this respect faithfully to the schema of normative primacy postulated by his evolutionary theory of history as a whole.[17] Developed in the late sixties, this conception has since

17. *Legitimation Crisis*, London 1976, especially pp. 75-94. For a telling critique of Habermas's conceptions here, see David Held, 'Crisis Tendencies, Legitimation and the State', in John Thompson and David Held, eds., *Habermas — Critical Debates*, London 1982, pp.181-195. This volume, which contains a wide range of contributions, starting with a fine essay by Agnes Heller, 'Habermas and Marxism', and concluding with a detailed and painstaking reponse by Habermas, is itself an admirable practical example of the discursive principles advocated by him. Note that in his 'Reply to my Critics', Habermas confesses that the 'evidential dimension' of the concept of truth in his epistemology is 'badly in need of further clarification' — while still attempting to scout empirical correspondence as a 'limit case', rather than a central criterion, of such truth: p.275.

received little empirical confirmation. If anything, the onset of world recession in the seventies has undermined the economic regulation of the major capitalist states, *without* generating any crisis in the legitimation of the market system as such. The outcome so far has been the reverse of that expected by Habermas: twelve million unemployed in the USA and UK alone, presided over — however — by reinvigorated governments of the Far Right, with Reagan and Thatcher at the helm. This failing — conceivably a provisional one — is in some ways perhaps less serious than the complete absence in Habermas's account of any collective *agency* for converting a delegitimation of the existing social order into an advance towards the new legitimacy of a socialist order. The problem of structure and subject is here, once again, posed in its most acute form on the terrain of practical politics itself.

Habermas too lacks any answer to the problem, as could be anticipated from the predisposition of his social theory as a whole towards the model of communication. But — and here is the decisive difference with structuralism, for all the shared limits of the common language model — what is striking is the consistency and fidelity of Habermas's commitment to his own version of a Frankfurt-style socialism, without wavering or somersault, over the past twenty-five years. That commitment was never a revolutionary one, and could not meet the shock of 1968. But nor was it overborn by the aftermath of that year. While many French intellectuals had made the journey from anarchism or Maoism to Cold War anti-communism by the end of the decade, Habermas stood firm against the repressive purges of the *Berufsverbot*, reaffirming his own form of allegiance to the legacy of Marx expressly against the current of the official drive to extirpate it as subversive from the Federal order. This divergence, inexplicable from within the logic of linguistic exorbitancy itself, refers us back to the political history in which it alone becomes intelligible.

Let me sum up my argument so far, as its strands now come together. I began by comparing the predictions that I made for the future of Marxism as a critical theory, in the early seventies, with its actual development since then. The balance-sheet, I argued, followed fairly closely some of the lines I had conjectured. Above all, Marxism had witnessed a simultaneous turn to the concrete and a spread to the

English-speaking world that together represented a remarkable renaissance of its intellectual vitality and international appeal. At the
same time, however, there were two striking deficits within this
overall accounting. One was topical: the failure of any truly strategic
discourse to emerge within the kind of historical materialism that
succeeded a predominantly philosophical Western Marxism proper.
The other was geographical: the sudden collapse of confidence and
morale within the zone of Latin culture, where Western Marxism had
been strongest in the post-war period. What were the reasons for this
regional 'crisis of Marxism' in Southern Europe? The superior powers
of structuralism, which at first glance seemed an obvious answer,
proved on inspection to be implausible — the chequered political
record of the latter emphasizing its dependence on an external context
it could not theorize. In Germany, which saw neither a qualitative
growth of Marxist culture of the Anglo-American type nor a precipitous
fall-back of the Franco-Italian kind, but rather the consolidation of a
traditionally strong production, very similar themes to those of structuralism were reworked in Habermas's attempt to reconstruct historical
materialism, yet coexisted with a quite distinct political stance. To
understand this intellectual pattern as a whole, across all three zones,
it is necessary to turn outwards to that far broader *extrinsic* history to
which Marxism has always accorded a provisional primacy of principle
in attempts to explain its own development.

So far in these lectures I have scarcely mentioned the largest single
reality that inevitably impinged on that development in the period we
have been considering. This was, of course, the fate of the international
communist movement. The Western Marxist tradition had always
been marked by a peculiar combination of tension and dependence in
its relation to it. On the one hand, this was a filiation which from its
very outset in the early twenties — as Russell Jacoby has recently well
reminded us[18] — had embodied hopes and aspirations for a developed
socialist *democracy* which the implacable machinery of bureaucratic
dictatorship crushed in the USSR with the rise of Stalin. However
mediated, sublimated or displaced — and it became all these in the
course of the next forty years — the ideal of a political order beyond

18. *Dialectic of Defeat*, Cambridge 1981, pp.61-62 ff.

capital that would be more, rather than less, advanced than the parliamentary regimes of the West, never deserted it. Hence the permanently critical distance of the Western Marxist tradition from the state structures of the Soviet Union — a distance which can even be discerned in the writings of those of its representatives closest to the international communist movement itself: at different times Sartre and Lukács, Althusser and Della Volpe, not to speak of Korsch or Gramsci or Marcuse. On the other hand, this tradition nearly always had a sense of the extent to which the Russian Revolution and its sequels, whatever their barbarities or deformities, represented the sole real breach with the order of capital that the twentieth century has yet seen — hence the ferocity of the onslaughts of the capitalist states against them, from the Entente intervention in the Russian Civil War, to the Nazi attack on the USSR, to the Korean War fought against China, to the attempted assault on Cuba, and then the war on Vietnam itself. In the West, moreover, the alternative tradition within the labour movement, that of social-democracy, had lost any force of real opposition to capitalism, becoming a generally servile prop of the status quo. There, the only militant adversaries the local bourgeoisies encountered continued to be Communist Parties ideologically bound to the USSR, where these existed as mass organizations. For all these reasons, the Western Marxist tradition was also typically oblique and prudent in its criticisms of the Communist states themselves. Direct and extended theoretical analysis of them in their own right was rarely if ever attempted — in significant contrast, of course, to the underground tradition descending from Trotsky, with its roots in the political struggles of the twenties in the Soviet Union. Herbert Marcuse's *Soviet Marxism* is an honourable exception, but even it is characteristically concerned with the ideology rather than the polity of the USSR.

This constitutive ambiguity of attitude in the Western Marxist tradition found its sharpest intellectual focus for a time in the work of one thinker, Jean-Paul Sartre. The reason for this lay in his peculiar position between the two dominant options within Western Marxism in the fifties: formal membership of a Communist Party, to be practically close to popular politics, at the price of theoretical silence *about* that politics (Lukács, Althusser or Della Volpe); or a distancing from any form of organizational commitment or commentary on current politics (the survivors of the Frankfurt School). Sartre, at the head of his journal *Les Temps Modernes*, never joined the French Communist Party; but he *did* try to develop a consequent practice of Marxist political intervention and theoretical interpretation of the course of the class struggle in France, and the world outside it. It was this project that brought him to the series of polemical essays on *The Communists and Peace*, to the rupture with Merleau-Ponty that arose out of it, to the famous articles on Stalinism of 1956-57, and then to the composition of the *Critique of Dialectical Reason* itself. I remarked yesterday that the abandonment of the second volume of the *Critique*, in the late fifties or early sixties, was a crucial moment in the intellectual history of post-war France. Part of the reason for this renunciation, certainly, lay in the intractable philosophical difficulties Sartre encountered when he started to try to construct what he called an 'enveloping totalization' of antagonist praxes that would found the unity of a 'plurality of conflicting epicentres of action'.[19] This was the

19. *Critique de la Raison Dialectique*, Vol. II (unpublished), mss. p.1. I have discussed the theoretical leakages in Sartre's programme in Volume II of the *Critique* in *Arguments Within English Marxism*, pp 52-53. These essentially lay in his attempt to construe the intelligibility of an entire historical epoch and social formation — the USSR from the 1930's to the 1950's — through the figure of Stalin as its final instance of unification: in other words, in a surreptitious *elision* of the distance between biography and history which the two parts of Volume I had in their own way acknowledged. We can now see how early Sartre's preoccupation with this problem was, and how strong was the pull towards this short-circuiting of it, from the recent publication of his Diaries of the Phoney War period, *Les Carnets de la Drôle de Guerre*, Paris 1983. This work, of unsurpassed vivacity and brilliance within his collected writings as a whole, contains anticipations of virtually every major theme of his post-war output. The most fascinating example of these is the long excursus on the historical personality of Kaiser Wilhelm II and his relation to the advent of the First World War, prompted by the outbreak of the Second: pp 357-375, 377-380, 383-387. After a virtuoso sketch of the socio-psychic making of the last of the Hohenzollerns, which announces every significant philosophical theme of his later study of Flaubert, Sartre concludes: 'All that I have tried to show is that it is conventional historical method and the psychological prejudices which govern it — not the structure of things itself — that generates the division of History into parallel layers of meaning. This parallelism disappears if one treats historical characters in the light of the unity of their historialization. But I accept that what I think I have demonstrated is only valid where the historical study in question is a *monograph* that shows the individual as the artisan of his own destiny. But of course he also acts *on others*. I will try in a few days time to reflect on Wilhelm II's share of "responsibility" for the war of 1914.' (pp 386-387.) Suggestively, this resolution was never kept, at least in those portions of the diaries that have survived.

decisive problem of the revolving relations between structure and subject, as we have seen. There is no doubt, from the manuscript, that Sartre lost his way here. But the colossal scale of his work on Flaubert would testify that his theoretical energies were far from exhausted. He could have returned to attack this theoretical crux with renewed vigour at a later date — as philosophers had done in analogous circumstances before him. The reason why he did not lies elsewhere in the unpublished mass of Volume II.

For what Sartre had attempted to do was to conduct his critical investigation through the medium of the actual historical processes that led from the October Revolution to the apotheosis of Stalin after the Second World War and beyond, in the Soviet Union. It is the class struggles and political conflicts of that long and bloody experience that form his dialectical laboratory. The choice was no mere hasard. Soon after the publication of the first volume of the *Critique*, Sartre remarked — when asked about the publication of the second — that as the sequel was about history itself, it would depend how that history turned out, 'what happened next'. The meaning of this cryptic reply becomes clear on a reading of the manuscript.[20] The real intellectual horizon of the *Critique* was political: Sartre's hope for a developing democratization of the USSR under Khrushchev expressed exactly that optimistic perspective on Soviet history as a whole so eloquently set out in his long essay of 1956, *The Ghost of Stalin*, which in and through its very excoriation of the Russian intervention in Hungary, held firm to the prediction that 'destalinization will destalinize the destalinizers'.[21] It was almost certainly the disappointment of this expectation by the early sixties which broke off the intention of the second volume.

From 1954 to 1960, Soviet society had appeared on the whole to be moving away from the mortmain of Stalin, as labour camps were dissolved, prisoners released, cultural life liberalized, economic reforms granted to benefit consumers and the countryside, and a new international policy of 'peaceful coexistence' proclaimed. Sartre looked forward to the radicalization of that process, with the recovery of direct sovereignty by the Russian working class and peasantry, amidst

20. Soon to be analysed at length by the American scholar Ronald Aronson.
21. *Situations VII*, Paris 1965, p.261.

revived political freedoms and secured personal rights. The failures of Khrushchev's last years — from the Cuban missile crisis to the disastrous harvests of the early sixties — led, in the event, in the opposite direction. Two decades of bleak Brezhnevite conservatism followed. There was to be one last experience, however, of a liberal and reforming Communism in Eastern Europe — one far more enlightened than that of Khrushchevism: the Prague Spring in Czechoslovakia. There, in a semi-Westernized industrial and cultural environment, with strong pre-war parliamentary traditions, a conscious and genuine effort came from within the ruling party to shed the carapace of bureaucratic domination, and progress towards a real producers' democracy. The destruction of that prospect, with the Warsaw Pact invasion of August 1968, finished off the cycle of de-stalinization in the Soviet bloc itself. Sartre's last political essay of weight — *The Socialism that Came in From the Cold*[22] — was an obituary of the Czechoslovak experiment. It is no accident that he thereafter lost his compass and never produced a major political statement again, his pronouncements in the seventies becoming ever more occasional and erratic.

Meanwhile, however, a new gravitational force was exercising a tidal pull on the Western Marxist culture of the late sixties and early seventies. The discredit of Khrushchev's model of reformism in the USSR created the conditions in which Mao's launching of an officially proclaimed 'cultural revolution' in China came to seem a superior form of rupture with the institutional inheritance of Stalinist industrialization and bureaucratization — one historically more advanced because more radical, in every sense. Abroad, Chinese foreign policy attacked diplomatic collusion with imperialist powers, calling for active solidarity with oppressed peoples in the Third World. At home, spontaneous mass action against bureaucratic privilege, from below, was stressed in lieu of cautious reforms from above; instead of greater space for market forces, social egalitarianism was exalted at all levels. Beyond class divisions themselves, the Cultural Revolution announced as its goal transcendence of the division between mental and manual labour itself, as well as the age-old division between town and country. All this was to be realized through direct popular administration in the

22. See *Between Existentialism and Marxism*, London 1974, pp.84-117.

spirit of the Paris Commune, and the unleashed energy and enthusiasm of the younger generation. The appeal of this ideological programme was very wide in the West, where it seemed to resonate from the other end of the world common themes of hostility to technocratic consumerism, educational hierarchy and parasitic over-industrialization. In Europe, Althusser was the most prominent and influential Marxist thinker to invest much of his hope for a democratic communism in the Maoist project in China. His Italian correspondent and collaborator Macciocchi became the author of one of the most unconditional encomia of it.[23] But the wave of sympathy and admiration for the Cultural Revolution swept up a very broad range of socialist intellectuals, not to speak of student militants: affecting in different degrees and different ways Dutschke and Enzensberger in Germany, Poulantzas, Glucksmann and Kristeva in France, Rossanda and Arrighi in Italy, Sweezy and Magdoff in the USA, Robinson and Caldwell in Britain.

The real substance and direction of the Maoist experience in China, however, was to prove very different from the ideal images which gained such diffusion abroad. Already by the early seventies, the momentum of an unrestrained anti-Soviet campaign — initially intelligible enough, then increasingly unbalanced and hysterical — led the Chinese state to an ever closer embrace with the United States government, and an ever more accentuated abandonment of support or solidarity for national liberation movements in the Third World, in exchange for amity with the most brutal and reactionary regimes across three continents, from Chile to Zaire, and Iran to Sudan. Domestically, it became increasingly clear that the Cultural Revolution was not only manipulated by the very bureaucratic summit it was ostensibly first aimed against, but in practice amounted to something very different from its declared goals: a gigantic purge of party and state apparatuses, involving a huge toll of political repression, with millions of victims; economic stagnation, as demographic pressures mounted; and ideological obscurantism, as every field of culture and education regressed in the irrationalism of a Mao cult surpassing that of Stalin himself. The final balance-sheet was far direr than that of

23. Maria-Antonietta Macciocchi, *Daily Life in Revolutionary China*, New York 1972.

Khrushchevism before it. Popular repudiation of the Cultural Revolution, after Mao's death, was overwhelming. The reaction to it, indeed, soon came to resemble in many of its features the pragmatic cast, at once liberal and cynical, of Khrushchevite reformism itself.

The impact of this sombre parabola on the tenor of the Western Marxism that followed it from afar was bound to be great. In the event, however, it was to be compounded by a second decisive experience of these years. The Cultural Revolution and its consequences had consummated the Eastern schism within the Soviet-dominated international communist movement. The advent of Eurocommunism a decade later effected a symmetrical Western schism. Its starting-point too was a critique of the legacy of Stalinism in the Soviet Union, and of the petrification of the prospect of internal reforms in the USSR and Eastern Europe. But whereas Maoism had reacted primarily against Khrushchevism, Eurocommunism — chronologically later and thematically distinct — was a response to the burial of it in the Brezhnevite consolidation of the sixties and seventies. Its real genesis dates from the invasion of Czechoslovakia, a Soviet action which was for the first time condemned with virtual unanimity by the West European Communist parties. The Eurocommunist alternative to the Russian model, as it crystallized towards the mid-seventies, laid central stress on the need to preserve the full range of civic liberties characteristic of capitalist democracy in any socialism to be achieved in the West, in a political order entrenching personal rights and plurality of parties alike, maintaining parliamentary institutions and repudiating any sudden or violent rupture with the private ownership of the means of production. In other words, it was a peaceful, gradual, constitutional road to socialism, antipodal to the model of the October Revolution and to the Bolshevik regime that emerged from it.

The attraction of these proposals to many of the survivors or heirs of Western Marxism was comprehensible enough. The adoption of Eurocommunist positions by the leaderships of the major Communist Parties of the West, above all, in Italy, France and Spain, could be seen as a belated official acceptance of the heterodox concern with socialist democracy which had underlain much of the Western Marxist tradition from the outset — its critique of the Soviet model finally rejoining that adumbrated by Korsch or Gramsci forty years earlier.

Two circumstances helped to make the adhesion of Marxist intellectuals to the Eurocommunist perspective an especially numerous one. Despite the deep differences in the content of the two scissions, Maoism and Eurocommunism representing in many ways polar ideological opposites, they shared a common point of negative reference in the USSR. Chinese propaganda had, by the mid-seventies, become obsessively and virulently anti-Soviet. China itself had by then lost much of its lustre abroad, but the Russophobia which it had diffused in the wide circles in Western Europe that had fallen under Maoist influence lingered on. In some cases, the result was simply a rapid transition to a conventional anti-communism *tout court* — the trajectory, essentially, of the French New Philosophers. But more frequent was an evolution from Maoism *to* Eurocommunism, mediated by the vehement rejection of the Soviet experience common to both. This movement was especially marked in France; Althusser, for all his initial misgivings at the dropping of the formula of the 'dictatorship of the proletariat' by the French Communist Party, was emblematic of it. A much more powerful factor in the general rallying to Eurocommunism, however, was the political situation in Southern Europe itself. Midway through the seventies, this whole region appeared ripe for popular advance and social change. In France, after nearly two decades of uninterrupted rule, the Right was sinking into discredit and division. In Italy Christian-Democratic corruption and incompetence were generating ever wider protest and larger electorates for the Italian Communist Party. In Spain, Portugal and Greece, fascist or military dictatorships were at the end of their tether. In all these countries, the Communist Parties were still the largest organizational force in the working class, either in legality or in the underground. The chance for a historic breakthrough, beyond the social stalemate of welfare capitalism in Northern Europe, appeared to be a real one, as the electoral expectation of coalition governments of the Left coincided with the ideological conversion to a specifically Western pluralism announced by Eurocommunism. Not since the end of the Liberation, it can be said, had such a fund of popular hope built up in broad masses of workers and intellectuals alike.

In the event, the outcome was uniformly dispiriting. One after the other, in one different way after another, the large Communist Parties missed their opportunities. The Italian Party wasted its substance in the fruitless pursuit of a junior partnership with the principal organization of the Italian bourgeoisie, the Christian-Democratic Party, disillusioning its supporters without winning the office it craved. The French Party, apprehensive of *its* social-democratic partner, broke up the Union of the Left when it was still a strong organization, precipitating electoral failure in 1978 — only to enter into government three years later, now enfeebled and subordinate, with the self-same social-democracy. The Portuguese Party, alone in rejecting Eurocommunism, unsuccessfully tried to seize power in a bureaucratic putsch, and ended the Portuguese Revolution in so doing. The Spanish Party, the central force in underground resistance to Franco's regime, rallied to the monarchy bequeathed by Franco, only to find itself marginalized and outnumbered by a Socialist Party that had been completely inactive during the dictatorship. These cumulative failures were a demoralizing blow to all those who had looked for a new dawn of the European labour movement in the passing of the old order in the South. It was here that the 'crisis of Marxism', so called, had its source and its meaning. Its real determinants had very little to do with its overt themes. What detonated it was essentially a *double disappointment*: first in the Chinese and then in the West European alternatives to the central post-revolutionary experience of the twentieth century so far, that of the USSR itself. Each of these alternatives had presented itself as a historically *new* solution, capable of overcoming the dilemmas and avoiding the disasters of Soviet history: yet each of their upshots proved to be a return to familiar deadlocks. Maoism appeared to debouch into little more than a truculent Oriental Khrushchevism. Eurocommunism lapsed into what looked increasingly like a second-class version of Occidental social-democracy, shamefaced and subaltern in its relation to the mainstream tradition descending from the Second International.

It was, of course, the latter disappointment that was the crucial one. It directly affected the conditions and perspectives of socialism within those advanced capitalist countries which had seemed till then to offer the most opportunities for real progress by the labour movement in the West. Here, then, we can see why the 'crisis of Marxism' was a quintessentially *Latin* phenomenon: for it was precisely in the three major Latin countries — France, Italy and Spain — that the chances of Eurocommunism seemed fairest, and the subsequent deflation was sharpest. The forms of that deflation have varied widely, from clamorous transfers to the right to mute exits from politics altogether. The most widespread pattern, however, has been a sudden shrinkage of socialist challenge and aspiration, now scaled down — with a bad conscience, and worse pretexts — to fit the crabbed accommodation of a new social-democracy to capitalism. Decked out as a fresh 'Euro-socialism', beneficiary of the falling away of Eurocommunism, the governments and parties of Mitterrand, Gonzalez and Craxi have since attracted the allegiance of most of the repentant and disabused, within a prospect of prudent reform at home and pronounced adherence to the 'Atlantic community' abroad.

The situation elsewhere was necessarily rather different. In Britain and the United States, West Germany and Scandinavia, there had never been mass Communist Parties to attract the same projections or hopes in the post-war period. In Northern — as opposed to Southern — Europe, social-democratic governments had been the norm for decades: reformist administration of capitalism held few novelties for the Marxism that had developed there since the sixties, whose main political focus was precisely a critique of it. In the United States, the effects of the Vietnam War were relayed, virtually without interruption, by those of the world recession, to create the context for a continuous growth of Marxist culture, from a very small starting-base, rather than a crisis of it. These conditions produced an environment affording little soil for collective conversions or collapses of the Gallic or Italian type. A steadier and more tough-minded historical materialism proved generally capable of withstanding political isolation or adversity, and of generating increasingly solid and mature work in and through them. This is not to say that analogous developments may not affect sectors of the Anglo-American or Nordic Lefts in the future. The popular consolidation of political regimes of imperialist reaction in Britain, or the United States, in the mid eighties may well break the nerve of some socialists, drawing them rightwards in an anxious quest for the middle ground. The extent of such possible responses, however, remains to be seen. For the moment, the contrast between the relative robustness and vitality of Marxism in this zone, and its corrosion and malady in the lands of the aborted Eurocmmunist experience, is stark enough.

Now, if the vicissitudes of Eurocommunism were the principal cause, displaced and concealed, of the disarray of Latin Marxism, they *also* provide the major explanation for the other central contradiction of that prospectus for the future of historical materialism with which I started. The one crucial area, it will be remembered, where little or no work corresponding to my predictions occurred, was that of Marxist *strategy*. My assumption had been that the resurgence of mass working-class and student militancy at the end of the sixties made possible, and foreseeable, the reunification of Marxist theory and popular practice that alone could generate the kind of revolutionary strategy that had been the achievement of classical Marxism in the epoch of the October Revolution, and whose absence had crippled Western Marxism for so long. What in fact happened was both near and far from this scenario. There was a major closing of the gap between Marxist theory and mass political practice, which had vital and fertile effects on the theory, but the circuit reuniting them was predominantly a *reformist* rather than a revolutionary one. The framework of my reflections in the mid-seventies had formally allowed for this variant, as one of a range of possible combinations, but their conclusion did not take it sufficiently into account. Eurocommunism did, for all its limitations, put practical questions of a transition to socialism in conditions of advanced capitalism on the agenda of Marxist theory. The apparent imminence of Left governments, with Communist participation, in France, Italy and Spain concentrated the minds of Marxist intellectuals powerfully, all across the West.

This development greatly contributed towards that turn to the concrete which, I have argued, has characterized the typical forms of historical materialism to succeed the principally philosophical tradition of Western Marxism proper. Political, economic and sociological analyses were now produced in abundance, where formerly there had been a notable dearth. But in the strategic field in the strict sense, little of value emerged. For while Eurocommunism presented itself as a 'third road', as its Italian spokesmen have called it, between Stalinism and Social-Democracy, its actual practice increasingly came to seem merely a repetition of the mournful route back into capitalism of the

Second International. No *new* strategic thought could arise along that journey. As to the areas outside the Eurocommunist arena, in Northern Europe or North America, no mass socialist movement of comparable dimensions has yet developed; there the landscape held few illusions, but also few possibilities as yet for directly confronting the problem of the overthrow of the authority of capital.

Nor, it must be said, did the alternative tradition of revolutionary Marxism, with its characteristically much greater strategic emphasis and insight — which had seemed to possess the potential for central contributions to any workable transition towards socialism in the West — prove significantly more fruitful than its historical rivals. The Marxist filiation descending from Trotsky appeared well poised, when I was writing *Considerations on Western Marxism,* to re-enter the post-Stalinized mass politics of the Left in the advanced capitalist countries, after decades of marginalization. Always far closer to the principal concerns of socialist practice, economic and political, than the philosophical line of Western Marxism, the distinctive theoretical heritage of the Trotskyist tradition gave it obvious initial advantages in the new conjuncture of popular upsurge and world depression, that marked the early seventies. Yet in the event, the promise it contained was not to be fulfilled in this period. The conceptions and evasions of Eurocommunism met their most effective critiques from the literature of Trotskyism. But although the polemical charge of texts like Ernest Mandel's *From Stalinism to Eurocommunism* left their object typically without riposte,[24] these negative demonstrations of the incoherence and implausibility of central Eurocommunist assumptions were not accompanied by any sustained positive construction of an alternative scenario for defeating capitalism in the West. The blockage stemmed from too close an imaginative adherence to the paradigm of the October Revolution, made against the husk of a feudal monarchy, and too distant a theoretical concern with the contours of a capitalist democracy the Bolsheviks never had to confront.

History presented one decisive experience to this movement in these years, but the test proved beyond its powers. The fall of

24. An oblique exception is perhaps to be found in the interesting exchange between Nicos Poulantzas and Henri Weber, 'The State and the Transition to Socialism', *Socialist Review*, March-April 1978, pp.9-37.

Portuguese fascism created the most favourable conditions for a socialist revolution in any European country since the surrender of the Winter Palace: a large electoral majority for the workers' parties in the (provisional) representative apparatuses of the state was here *combined* with the decomposition of the (inherited) repressive apparatuses of the state, and the emergence of major insurgent sectors in the officer corps and rank-and-file of the armed forces, resolved to force a passage to socialism. A dual opportunity of this sort has never arisen elsewhere, under conditions of advanced capitalism. The Portuguese Communist Party, vainly attempting to repeat the Czechoslovak road to bureaucratic power of 1948, inevitably missed it. But so too did the small Trotskyist movement operating on its flanks. Although it produced the sharpest and most interesting internal debate of the decade on the course of the Portuguese process,[25] it also failed to synthesize the contending positions, each with its contradictory share of truth, into any cogent or innovative strategy. The Fourth International lost its way at the cross-roads of the Portuguese Revolution, as the uncertain groupings of subsequent years were to show. The dearth of strategic resource or invention — agencies and occasions, projections and surprises, forms and demands, organizations and initiatives, ways and means in their totality capable of surpassing and evicting the order of capital — was not to be seriously remedied, from any quarter, in this period.

The problem of such a strategy remains today, as it has done now for fifty years, the Sphinx facing Marxism in the West. It is clear that the freedom of capitalist democracy, meagre but real with its ballot or bill of rights, can only yield to the force of a qualitatively greater liberty of socialist democracy, exercised over work and wealth, economy and family as well as polity. But how are the supple and durable structures of the bourgeois state, endlessly elastic in adjustment of the consent on which it immediately rests and infinitely rigid in preservation of the coercion on which it ultimately relies, to be overpowered? What bloc of social forces can be mobilized, in what ways, ever to undertake the *risks* of disconnecting the cycle of capital accumulation in our intricately integrated market economies? These are questions that remind us, again and again, that the problem of

25. See the official files of *Inprecor* for 1974-1975, *passim*.

structure and subject — structures of operative economic and political power, subjects of any calculable insurgency against them — is one not only for critical theory but also for the most concrete of all practices.

I do not wish to end on a resumptive note, however, but on an expectant one. The issues just discussed are ones I argued were central, nearly a decade ago. Yet there are others, also in need of exploration, which I did not then raise. For if the moment of power is the alpha of any serious Marxist problematic, it is not the omega. *For what ends*, in the names of what values and ideals, could a social movement be imaginably inspired to struggle against the dominion of advanced capital in the world today? Here I will hasard the prediction that the major challenge to Marxism as a critical theory in the next decades will come from a very different direction from the one reviewed here, and that it is on the terrain of that challenge that it will have to develop its omega. In a memorable phrase, Frank Lentricchia has spoken of the 'stereophonic sirens of idealism'[26] that have seduced so many in recent years. Structuralism, among other things, was certainly that — an immensely alluring form of idealism. My guess however, is that a more powerful intellectual challenge will in future come from *naturalism*. The signs of this are all around us, I think — variable syntheses of them perhaps waiting just over the horizon. Traditionally, and especially in the Anglo-American cultures, an emphasis on biological determinants of social realities has always been associated with the Right. That lineage has been newly reinforced with the advent of so-called sociobiology as such — itself derivative from the relatively recent discipline of ethology, each in turn falling into position within a long-standing behaviourism that preceded them. The ideological drift of this tradition has always been a reactionary conception of human nature, understood as a permanent physiological nexus narrowly restricting all possible social choice. The nature in question is invariably at once aggressive and conservative, individualist yet inertial — a standing warning against radical experiment or revolutionary change.

26. *After the New Criticism*, Chicago 1980, p.208: an especially apt phrase, as it happens, for the hi-fi swooning noted above.

The Left has always fought these ideas of an eternal, unamenable human nature, in the name of the social *variability* of human beings under different historical orders, and their *ameliorability* under conditions that emancipate rather than oppress them. Recently, however, it is noticeable that writers of either socialist or left-liberal persuasion have increasingly tended to argue for another version of human nature itself: of what one might call a *protective*, rather than *restrictive* type. The outstanding American examples are Noam Chomsky and Barrington Moore. Their common theme, it might be said, is a certain notion of natural autonomy or creativity in human beings. Chomsky maintains that political ideas 'must be rooted ultimately in some conception of human nature and human needs'. In his view 'the fundamental human capacity is the need for creative self-expression, for free control of all aspects of one's life and thought'; whereas 'if humans are just plastic and random organisms, then why not control that randomness by the state authority or the behavioural technologist?'[27] Moore's position is somewhat more pessimistic, but clearly related. For him, minimal conceptions of justice — what he calls standards of 'decent treatment' — are universals of human nature;[28] but sufficiently powerful mechanisms of social mystification or coercion can induce an amnesia — not obliteration — of them, of the sort that Chomsky would fear. Moore's study of *Injustice* consequently allows for both fixity and variability in human responses to social organization. Neither Chomsky nor Moore, of course, are Marxists. But within Marxism itself, the powerful work of the Italian philologist Sebastiano Timpanaro has long defended another variant of human nature on the Left — what could be called, to distinguish it, a *privative* conception, which insists sheerly and eloquently on the biological limits of all human life, whether of the individual or of the species, in disease, decrepitude and death.[29] The function of this naturalism in all three writers is to found an *ethics*. The notorious absence of anything approaching such an ethics within the accumulated corpus of historical

27. Linguistics and Politics — an Interview', *New Left Review*, No.57, September-October 1969, pp.31-32.

28. Barrington Moore Jr. *Injustice: the Social Bases of Obedience and Revolt*, New York 1978, pp.5-13.

29. *On Materialism*, pp.29-72.

materialism — its regular displacement by either politics or aesthetics — lends this project a peculiar point and force.

In each case, of course, difficult questions arise — essentially those posed by the *relation* between nature, so conceived, and history. It is the articulation of these two terms that poses — I would argue — the other great crux for Marxism as a critical theory, comparable to that of the relation between structure and subject. The same problem re-appears nearly everywhere along the symptomatic frontiers of the traditional concerns and conceptions of historical materialism, where new political movements or issues outside its classical perimeter have now become unevadable. The three most obvious examples of these are the questions of women, ecology and war. What are the reasons for the immemorial oppression of women — as near to a sociological universal, in class and pre-class societies alike, as anthropology can vouchsafe us? Polemic over the question rages to this day within the women's movement — necessarily so, since it governs the future forms of women's emancipation. At one pole, radical feminists like Firestone have opted for a wholesale biologism, if in the end a desperately mutable one. At the other, theorists of gender construction virtually deny any natural basis to the sexual division of labour at all. Yet even the most unremitting anti-naturalist account of sexual in-equality must still be able to explain why *biological* differences should have been selected for the construction of social divisions. The articulation of nature and history is uneludable.

If it is true that the dominant trend in the women's movement today tends to tilt the relationship too unilaterally in a culturalist direction, the opposite trend is surely predominant in the ecological movement, in which outer and inner nature often acquire a metaphysical fixity and identity well beyond any materialist conception of the range of their historical variations. Still, the problems of the interaction of the human species with its terrestrial environment, essentially absent from classical Marxism, are unpostponable in their urgency. One of the distinctive virtues of the Frankfurt tradition was its awareness of this, at whatever a philosophical level of reflection. In different registers, Raymond Williams and Rudolf Bahro have centrally addressed these issues, and it is no accident that in each case the question of the acceptable or unacceptable meanings of nature *in* humanity is immediately thrown up by that of the acceptable or unacceptable relations of humanity *to* nature.[30] History and nature are necessarily reconjugated in every ecological discussion.

Finally, and most fatefully of all, the possibility of global nuclear war, destroying all forms of life on earth, presents for the first time the deadly, proximate threat of a common terminus of the two: the end of human history in the extinction of animate nature. The very thought of such a contingency would have been unimaginable to the founders of historical materialism; its reality thus imposes entirely new problems for any critical theory that attempts to look the close of the twentieth century in the face. Here too, it is no chance that current mediations or conjectures on the dynamics that have led to the increasingly dangerous international field of forces that we witness today, and which promises worse dangers of proliferation and tension tomorrow, should have resorted to naturalist speculations. Edward Thompson and Régis Debray — two very contrasted thinkers, yet each once of committed Marxist background — have recently converged in proposing a virtually ontological dialectic of Self and Other, transhistorically inherent in collective human bonding as such, as the ultimate explanation of the multiplying national hatreds and escalating international arms race of the post-war world.[31] All such notions will have to be very carefully, and coolly, examined. What they tell us, however, is that if the relations between structure and subject are the province par excellence of socialist strategy, the relations between nature and history bring us to the long overdue moment of socialist morality. Marxism will not complete its vocation as a critical theory unless and until it can adequately meet it.

30. Williams, *Problems in Materialism and Culture*, pp.67-122; Bahro, *Socialism and Survival*, London 1982, e.g. pp.24-43.

31. Compare Thompson, *Zero Option*, London 1982, pp 170-188 with Debray, *Critique of Political Reason*, London 1983, pp.298-345.

Postscript

There remains a final question that no attempt to take stock of the situation of Marxism today can avoid. What is the nature of the relationship between Marxism and socialism? There is a simple and classical answer to this: the one designates a theory capable of leading to what the other designates as a society. Such a reply, however, manifestly short-circuits the actual complexities and ambiguities of the connections between the two. For 'socialism' is not just the practical terminus of a historical process, waiting for us over the horizon. It is also an ideal movement of principles and values, sustained by passion and argument, active and unfolding in the present, and with nearly two centuries of a past behind it. In this sense socialism represents a cultural and political field of force that both precedes and exceeds Marxism. Theory itself, in this respect, is no monopoly of historical materialism: there were socialist thinkers of moment before Marx, and there have been since Marx, whose work bears little or no direct relationship to its intellectual framework. It would be a presumption to identify the two; there is obviously no complete coincidence between them. Recently, indeed, Edward Thompson has sought not only to distinguish, but to counterpose them quite sharply — dispensing with the cognitive pretensions of 'marxism' while reaffirming the moral claims of 'communism', in an eloquent plea for a new utopianism. The difficulty with such a position, however, is that it affords no ready account of why Marxism should have assumed the overwhelming salience it has in fact acquired in the international labour movement in this century. Here, once again, the demands of reflexivity with which we started need to be respected. It must be asked: what have been the historical grounds of the overall dominance of historical materialism within socialist thought and culture as a whole? More exactly: *in what* does the unique character of Marxism as a theory for a socialist lie — and *how far* does it extend?

Any response here must be somewhat stenographic in form. But very approximately, it might be said that the structural primacy of historical materialism on the Left to date has rested on three hallmarks that separate it from all other contributions to the culture of socialism. (i) The first is its sheer scope as an *intellectual system*. While there have been many other socialist thinkers of interest and merit, from Saint-Simon to Morris, from Jaurès to Wigforss, from Chayanov to Myrdal, only Marx and Engels produced a comprehensive body of theory capable of continuous, cumulative development after them. That capacity derived, of course, from the synthesis they achieved between 'German philosophy, British economics and French politics', as Lenin put it, which yielded a stock of inter-related concepts and theses covering a wider range of social forms and practices than any alternative could begin to meet. In this sense, there have been no equals or even potential rivals within socialism. There are other, individual socialist thinkers: there is, so far, only one corpus of socialist *thought* that constitutes a genuine collective paradigm of research — permitting inter-connected debates and exchanges across generations and continents, within a common language. (ii) The second peculiar power possessed by Marxism, within the broader compass of socialist thought, has always lain in its character as a *theory of historical development*. Here too, there have been many good socialist historians of other persuasions — Tawney or Lefebvre, Beard or Taylor. But there is only one contender as a general account of human development across the centuries from primitive societies to present forms of civilization. That is historical materialism. All other partial versions are derivations, or fragments, by contrast. Marxism alone has produced at once a sufficiently general and sufficiently differential set of analytic instruments to be able to integrate successive epochs of historical evolution, and their characteristic socio-economic structures, into an intelligible narrative.[1] In this respect, indeed, it remains unchallenged not only within socialist, but also non-socialist culture

1. For some suggestive reflections on the narrative instance in historical materialism, see Jameson, *The Political Unconscious*, pp 19-20.

as a whole. There is no competing story. Weber's work comes nearest to one, but for all the extraordinary richness of its particular investigations, it significantly falls short of any general dynamic, or principles of motion: subsequent attempts to deduce one from it, in banalized theories of 'modernization', have done no more than hollow out the wealth of Weber's erudition, leaving a vacant tautological shell behind. (iii) Thirdly, Marxism has stood apart from every other tradition of socialist thought in the effect of its radicalism as a *political call to arms*, in the struggle against capitalism. There have been competing trends within the labour movement in principle as intransigently militant, in the past — Spanish anarchism, for example; but without efficacy as movements of social transformation. There have also been trends of considerable practical efficacy, such as Swedish social-democracy in its heyday; but without any radicalism of achievement. Capitalism has fallen to the forces fighting against it only where Marxism has risen to dominance among them. All successful socialist revolutions to date have been guided by, or rallied to, the banner of historical materialism.

These three faculties have not deserted Marxism to this day. But they are no cause for triumphalism. In many ways, historical materialism as a rational body of thought, informing a controlled practice of social change, has suffered from its very preeminence within the intellectual universe of socialism. As a theory, it has been — one might say — *too* powerful for its own good. Precisely because of its inordinate assets, its marginalization of contestants from the Left was often unduly easy, its victory over critics from the Right unprofitably cheap. For long, Marxism was never confronted with any really major intellectual challenges within the socialist movement, or indeed with any account of the great hinges in history of comparable solidity or confidence outside it.[2] The result could only be to perpetuate its areas of weakness. Knowledge rarely grows without an adequate coefficient

2. The abundance of more or less ritual denunciations of Marxism in Cold War manuals has never yielded anything of much pertinence: the latest, and in many ways one of the crudest, of these compendia is Leszek Kolakowski's *Main Currents of Marxism*, Oxford 1978. For the very different character of a genuine theoretical engagement, from an alternative sociological framework, see Anthony Giddens's *A Contemporary Critique of Historical Materialism*, London 1982, and the response to it by Erik Olin Wright, 'Giddens's Critique of Marxism', *New Left Review*, No 138, March-April 1983, pp 11-35. It is this kind of confrontation that has been unduly rare.

of resistance. Marxism has been the victim of its own advantages, very often: developing certain characteristic inertias and vices for want of proper corrections and counter-weights to it.

These advantages are, however, coming under a new pressure today — a change that can only be welcomed. Each of the traditional privileges of historical materialism, in fact, is now facing a significant challenge. Firstly, and most obviously, the systematicity of Marxism as a comprehensive theory of society has been put in question by the rise of the women's movement, developing discourses on the family or sexuality that escape much of its traditional scope altogether. The classical literature of Marxism did, of course, contain a memorable chapter devoted to these issues, in the work of the later Engels: but this was never consolidated into a continuous and central concern thereafter, lapsing into endemic neglect or deferral. Thus, even if the contradictions and omissions of that heritage have in part been made good by precarious resort to less scientific bodies of thought like psychoanalysis, there can be no doubt of the salutary and radical nature of the perceptual switch — the irreversible optical alteration — that the new feminism has brought about. The more strictly historical preeminence of Marxism is rather less threatened so far, although here too the emergence of a vigorous women's history is potentially a critical test for it. Beyond this, the signal importance of demography as an entirely unmastered, indeed largely unexplored, domain of history for Marxism is another cause for future perturbance within it, the effect of whose stimulus — when the full measure of it is taken — we have yet to see.[3] In general, it is noticeable that recent years have seen the successful establishment of a journal of *socialist* (not Marxist) historians in the English-speaking world, drawing on a wide range of international contributors — a new category.[4]

Thirdly, and finally, the kind of political radicalism once the peculiar property of Marxism has become dimmed by the progressive tarnishing of the image of the Communist states in the East, and the increasing integration of the Communist parties in the West into the conventional constitutional frameworks of capitalism. The twin failures of

3. A pioneering sortie into this territory can b. found in Wally Seccombe, 'Marxism and Demography', *New Left Review*, No 137, January-February 1983, pp 22-47.

4. *History Workshop Journal*, founded in 1976.

Khruschevism and Maoism, as attempts to reform the official structures of Russia and China, leaving behind them a long stalemate of mutual tension and suffocation of popular liberties, have had drastic effects upon the reputation of the doctrine in the name of which they are justified. But these in turn have been compounded by the dull conformism and domestic paternalism, sustenance of bourgeois sovereignty without and maintenance of bureaucratic authority within, of so many Eurocommunist parties that still invoke the memory of Marxism. None of these historical constellations is destined to last forever: but while they do, the fronts of real political insurgency in the advanced capitalist countries, at least, are liable to undergo significant displacements. The European peace movement, well to the left of the major Communist parties in the militancy of its methods and the radicalism of its goals, is already a sign of them.

This example, however, poses another question. The relationship between Marxism and socialism is one within a common intellectual field: it essentially concerns issues of theoretical enquiry. But it has also to be asked: what is the relationship between socialism itself, as a practice, and the process of human emancipation at large? Can these two be simply identified, towards the close of the twentieth century? Here again, it is the emergence of a radical and international movement for women's liberation that has posed the issue most directly. What connection is there between the abolition of sexual inequality and the advent of a classless society? The difficulty of any simple equation of the two does not lie so much in the persistence of male privilege, over a wide range of social life, in the post-revolutionary societies of today: for these transitional orders are not yet, by a long measure, definable in Marxist terms as socialist — while at the same time they do typically reveal significantly greater advances towards equality than pre-revolutionary societies, either recently industrialized or still agrarian, at comparable stages of economic development. The real problem for any straightforward integration of socialist and feminist perspectives is rather to be found in the nature and structure of capitalism.

For it is perfectly clear that the social domination of men over women long pre-dates capitalism — indeed is virtually coextensive with the history, not only recorded but even inferrable, of the species itself. No known primitive society today is other than asymmetrical in its distribution of power and position between the sexes. The early capitalist mode of production inherited and reworked this millenial inequality, with all its myriad oppressions, at once extensively utilizing and profoundly transforming it. In the course of its subsequent evolution, however, there can be no question but that it has on the whole mitigated rather than accentuated the toll of limitation and loss suffered by the second sex at the hands of the first. The elementary indices of labour, literacy and legality — work, culture and citizenship — have all moved in one direction only. Is there any necessary stopping-point for this process, within the boundaries of capital? The persistence of massive discrimination, in daily and public life alike, rooted in family, occupational and educational structures, is no conclusive argument against the formal compatibility of sexual equality and private property of the means of production: measurable progress has, after all, also been realized under late capitalism, and is still continuing. Economically, the pure mechanisms of the process of valorization of capital, and the expansion of the commodity form, are gender-blind. The logic of profit is indifferent to sexual difference. Even while existing bourgeois societies depend for their cultural and political stability in some calculable degree on the persistence of the traditional family, and therewith femininity, capitalism as a mode of production is in principle conceivable with an equalization — even reversal — of current masculine and feminine roles, at a higher level of abundance. Classes could still subsist, differentially related to the means of production, without nuclear families or gender barriers within them.

But is this a practical prospect? It is not, for one fundamental and unalterable reason. Sexual domination is much older historically, and more deeply rooted culturally, as a pattern of inequality, than class exploitation. To detonate its structures would require a far greater egalitarian charge, of collective psychic hopes and energies, than would be necessary to level the difference between classes. But if that charge ever exploded within capitalism, it is inconceivable that it could leave the — more recent and relatively more exposed — structures of class inequality standing. The blast from the one would inevitably sweep away the other. Any movement that incarnated values capable of realizing a society without hierarchy of gender would be constitutively incapable of accepting one founded on division of class. In that· sense, the rule of capital and the emancipation of women are — historically, and practically — irreconcilable.

Could such a scenario ever occur? That is, could the struggle against sexual domination ever provide the main impetus for a wider human liberation, tidally sweeping class struggle along with it to a common victory? The answer is plainly no. The reasons for that impossibility take us directly to the paradoxes of the relationship between socialism and feminism. For if the structures of sexual domination stretch back longer, and go deeper, culturally than those of class exploitation, they also typically generate less collective resistance, politically. The division between the sexes is a fact of nature: it cannot be abolished, as can the division between classes, a fact of history. After capitalist and worker have long vanished, women and men will remain. The biological differences that define the two sexes, moreover, render them interdependent on each other, so long as the species subsists: if abolition of the sexes is impossible, so too is their separation. Those reciprocal needs each have of the other which comprise a constant across human history, in and through the wide diversity of social guises they have assumed, have always ensured that the rules and mechanisms of masculine domination have been accompanied by forms and degrees of feminine compensation that have no strict equivalent in the economic relationships between the immediate producers and those who appropriate their product. Without this dialectic, the larger part of the history of human affections would be unimaginable. The ties so formed, of sentiment and support, within many of the very customs and practices of inequality themselves, have ordinarily also been sustained by the rough common equality of material condition that has so often (not always) prevailed between sexual partners within any given class themselves.[5]

Finally, and most crucially, just because of this pattern the immediate objects of resistance, or revolt, within the system of sexual

5. For a delicate and moving portrait of relationships between the sexes, which exemplifies these points, in a near-stone-age society with very pronounced structures of male domination, see Maurice Godelier's *La Production des Grands Hommes — Pouvoir et Domination Masculine chez les Baruya de Nouvelle-Guinée*, Paris 1982, pp 221-251 — a work by a Marxist scholar that will undoubtedly take its place among the classics of modern anthropology.

domination will often normally tend to be individual — since it is within the inter-sexual norms of conjugality or family that oppression has always been most intimately and durably exercised. Workers will characteristically rebel against their employers, or the state, collectively: class struggle is social or it is nothing. Women do not possess either the same positional unity or totalized adversary. Divided by economic class themselves, within their class dependent on men dependent on them, their forces are generally more molecular and dispersed, the point of concentration of their effort as liable to be a particular partner as a general gender. The peculiarity of the feminine condition within male-dominated societies can be seen, in this respect, from the absence of any specialized agencies for the regulation or repression of women: that is, any equivalent to the coercive apparatus of the State on the plane of social class. That is why, of course, tribal societies, without class or state, can still perfectly well enforce every degree of sexual inequality, from the relatively mild to the drastically severe. There is never any overall *centralization* of the structures of women's oppression: and this diffusion of it critically weakens the possibility of unitary insurgence against it. Without a centripetal focus for opposition, collective solidarity and common organization are always more difficult to achieve, more friable to maintain. None of this means, of course, that joint action by women for their liberation is impossible. On the contrary, it can be said that in the past decade such action has won a greater measure of advance than has any workers' struggle in the West. That has been true not only in terms of legal change or cultural attitude, but also in a more radical sense: the challenge from the women's movement since the 70's has probably done more than any other phenomenon to force some contemplation of the idea of a qualitatively different future into a becalmed bourgeois society.

But a critical distinction remains. Universal though the cause of women's emancipation may be, one so radical that men too will be freed from their existing selves by it, it is insufficiently operational as a collective agency, actual or potential, ever to be able to uproot the economy or polity of capital. For that, a social force endowed with another strategic leverage is necessary. Only the modern 'collective labourer', the workers who constitute the immediate producers of any

industrial society, possess that leverage — by reason of their specific
'class capacity', or structural position within the process of capitalist
machinofacture as a whole, which they alone can paralyze or transform; just as they alone, by reason of their potential cohesion and
mass, can furnish the central contingents of the organized army of
popular will and aspiration required for any decisive confrontation
with the bourgeois state. That army will, of course, include many
workers who are women themselves — ever more so, as the composition of the labour force continues to change away from its traditional sexual imbalance in the years to come; just as it will also include
feminists as well as socialists, mustered under their own banners. Any
insurgent bloc capable of unleashing a transition to socialism will be
various and plural in composition: but it will only be such, something
more than a mere collation of dissent, if it possesses a centre of gravity
in those who directly produce the material wealth on which the society
of capital is founded.

The tension between universality of goal and specificity of effect,
inscribed in the relationship between the practical causes of feminism
and socialism today, is in fact one visible in the original theoretical
succession from 'utopian' to 'scientific' socialism itself. The utopianism of Saint-Simon, Fourier or Owen accorded a far more lucid and
consistent attention to the disharmony of the sexes, and sought more
persistently and boldly to imagine ways to remedy it, than the thought
of Marx and Engels that eventually so largely supplanted it. Engels
could retrospectively 'delight in the stupendously grand thoughts and
germs of thought that everywhere break out through their fantastic
covering'[6] in the writing of these predecessors: but there is no exact
equivalent for the direction of many of them in the corpus of historical
materialism. It is no accident that contemporary feminists should
have turned back to the utopians so warmly, for continuity and
inspiration in their own work.[7] There is no question of the loss, of
political emphasis and imagination, that accompanied the general

6. *Anti-Dühring*, Moscow 1954, p 356.
7. See now the outstanding work of Barbara Taylor, *Eve and the New Jerusalem*,
London 1983, which admirably recovers for us the record of Owenite feminism, in all
its pungency and passion, and also explores the historical reasons for its subsequent
eclipse (a less absolute one, in the later 19th century, than conventional accounts have
rendered it).

codification of post-utopian socialism at the turn of the 20th century. But at the same time, it is necessary to see equally clearly why the utopian tradition was so quickly eclipsed. Presenting itself as a programme for the ethical reformation of humanity as a whole, it lacked any historical 'operator' to *shift* the enormous weight of material misery it so fervently denounced. Precisely because it sought to deliver the human race 'all at once' from bondage, it could explore issues of sex as much as, or more than, issues of class; but for the same reason it had no way of locating the lines of division *within* humanity capable of bringing about the new civilization. Its irenic universalism — the gospel of a secular religion as its founders formulated it[8] — precluded social conflict as a central principle of political change: hence its necessary resort to moral conversion as a substitute for it. The decisive advance of 'scientific' socialism was to break this deadlock by identifying the site of a particular social agency, rooted in historically specific forms of economic production, as the Archimedean point from which the old order could be overturned — the structural position occupied by the industrial working-class created by the advent of capitalism. That process, by definition, involved the sharpest bisection of society into opposite political camps, and endemic war between them. The gain that was registered by this transformation of perspective was so immense that it consigned the previous utopian problematic to virtual oblivion within socialist thought, for a long period. But there was a price to be paid for it: the narrowing of the characteristic range of concerns of Marxism as the dominant ideology of the labour movement in the 20th century.

The same divergence is posed today by the other, even greater, issue overflowing traditional channels of socialist thought — the prospect of nuclear war. Here too, but far more dramatically and finally, universal human interests, transcending the struggle between capital and labour, are at stake: nothing less than the survival of humanity itself. It is quite logical, then, that those who have done more than most to rouse a new peace movement into being, sounding

8. For an illuminating analysis of these and related traits of utopian socialism, see Gareth Stedman Jones, 'Utopian Socialism Reconsidered', in Raphael Samuel (ed), *People's History and Socialist Theory*, London 1981, pp 138-142. Symptomatically Owen's last significant political project was, of course, called the 'Association of All Classes of All Nations'.

the alarm at the constantly increasing risks of global annihilation, should also so often have called for a revival of the utopian heritage within socialism. Edward Thompson and Rudolf Bahro are outstanding examples. Each has felt a moral insufficiency within Marxism to contend with the shape of the danger now facing any future for humankind at all — an insensibility grounded in its nature as a theory of struggle between classes, pitting antagonistic forces without respite against each other, rather than of redemption of the species as a whole, as 'the bloodshot twentieth century lurches towards its end'.[9] Against this legacy, they have appealed for an *immediate* universalism, in a common human reflex — beyond the barriers of country and class alike — to ward off the threat of thermonuclear extinction.

The power, and rationale, of this appeal are incontestable. Businessman and worker, bureaucrat and peasant, will perish alike in any global war today. International peace is the condition for the pursuit of any form of socialism, just as it is for the preservation of any form of capitalism. The widest conceivable mobilization is needed today, and will be more urgent than ever tomorrow, against the gathering momentum of the nuclear arms race. But here too, on a planetary scale, the relationship between aim and agency is disjunctive. The benefits of arresting the drive towards a general conflagration can only be universal: but the forces capable of securing them will necessarily remain particular. The prolonged momentum of the Cold War that has led to the present deteriorating pass in international relations does not derive from inherited faults or warps within the moral constitution of humanity, as any neo-utopian diagnosis inevitably tends to suggest. It is the awful, but intelligible product of precisely that global class struggle whose understanding gave birth to historical materialism — a conflict founded on the ceaseless determination of major capitalist states to stifle every attempt to build socialism, from the Russian to the Vietnamese, the Central European down to the Central American revolutions, and the deformities the resistance to it has wrought

---

9. For Thompson's powerful analysis of the present war dangers, see his two essays 'Notes on Exterminism — The Last Stage of Civilization', and 'Europe, the Weak Link in the Cold War', pp1-34 and 329-349, in *Exterminism and Cold War*, London 1982, a volume which contains a wide range of international contributions discussing contemporary issues of the peace movement.

within them.[10] The potential outcome of this conflict transcends the opposition between capital and labour: but its actual springs remain tightly coiled within it. It is for that reason, too, that while the dominant classes in the West could foreseeably *yield* to measures of disarmament, on a rational calculation of the risks and costs of indefinite nuclear stock-piling, they will never be the *initiators* of any movement towards a denuclearized peace. The only political agencies capable of wrenching humanity away from the long-term run towards war lie to the side of labour, not capital — the dispossessed, rather than the possessors, of the fundamental means of production and coercion in the imperialist societies of today. There is no space, geometrical or historical, in which the categories of Right and Left can be magically sublated. Peace itself, so long as it signifies no more than the (negative) absence of war, is unlikely ever to mobilize the depths of patience or the heights of enthusiasm necessary to win it, among great masses of men and women all over the world, in the teeth of the sinister lull that passes for peace today. The positive outline of a social order beyond both capital and bureaucracy, which alone would lay to rest the menace of war between them, is the only realistic horizon for a peace movement that can endure. In Williams's words, 'To build peace, now more than ever, it is necessary to build more than peace'.[11]

In this respect, the two causes of general emancipation just considered have not wholly dissimilar ties with the specific cause of socialism itself. Neither is identical with it. But in each case the route to one passes through the other, as its probable condition. Without the supersession of classes, there is small chance of the equalization of sexes; just as without the dismantling of capital, there is little likelihood of the banishment of nuclear war. The peace movement and the women's movement are, in their practical fate, in the long-run indissociable from the dynamic of the labour movement. That gives no superior rights to the latter: the autonomy of the two critical forces of our time that pose directly universal demands requires absolute respect. But it does impose new responsibilities on the labour move-

10. For amplification of these points, see the fundamental essays by Mike Davis, 'Nuclear Imperialism and Extended Deterrence', and Fred Halliday, 'The Sources of the New Cold War', in *Exterminism and Cold War*, pp 35-64 and 389-328.

11. 'The Politics of Nuclear Disarmament', *Exterminism and the Cold War*, p 85.

ment. These include not only a material solidarity with the struggle for peaceful coexistence between nations, and for full equality between sexes, but also an ideal capacity to reconstruct and develop the idea of socialism itself, so that it can genuinely act as a fulcrum between them.

The urgency of this task is now plain. In recent years the very notion of socialism as an alternative form of civilization has become effaced and remote within broad masses of the working-class in the West, and fallen into popular discredit in significant zones of the East. In these conditions, it is all the more necessary to put a quite renewed emphasis on socialism as a *future society*, that exists nowhere in the world today, or even seems very close, yet whose articulated form it is essential to debate at once as boldly and as concretely as possible. The field of such debate is already discernible in the contrasts of current contributions to it, emphasising the opposite axes of values and institutions. To take the two most paradigmatic examples, on the one hand Edward Thompson has exalted the faculties of the utopian imagination as such, in figurations of moral desire freed from any too mundane calculus of conventional cognition; while on the other hand Raymond Williams has reproached the classical utopian impulse for tending towards an escapist simplification of the existing world, and insisted on the more exacting need for feasible institutional specification of any socialist future beyond it, which will always involve *greater* — not less — complexity than the arrangements of the capitalist present.[12] Were they pitted against each other, anarchism and fabianism would be the logical conclusion of either emphasis on its own. An open and inventive marxism should find its province in a flexible balance between them.

In fact, on the contrary, historical materialism has been taxed with deficiencies from both directions at once: as subject to a critique *by* utopianism, for the utilitarian narrowness of its compass of political concerns, and as subject to a critique *for* utopianism, in the impractical vagueness of its proposals for social change. Recent work by Carmen

---

12. See the contrasting comments on Morris in Thompson, *William Morris — from Romantic to Revolutionary* (revised edition), London 1977, pp 802-807; and Williams, *Problems in Materialism and Culture*, pp 202-205.

Sirianni contains a powerful example of the second type of argument.[13]
Of the two, each of which possesses its own measure of truth, it is
nevertheless the latter that has more force. Classical Marxism was in
general always sceptical towards 'blue-prints' of a socialist or communist future. But the vacuum left by its abstention from them could
not remain entirely unfilled: what took their place was, in effect,
untransformed residues of the tradition of utopian socialism itself,
which were never thoroughly criticized or reworked in the mature
writings of Marx or Engels, or their successors. The result was the
persistence, within a socialism that sought to be scientific, of such
themes — taken over *tel quel* from Saint-Simon — as the 'replacement
of the government of men by the administration of things', or — from
Fourier — of the 'abolition of the division of labour', which virtually
ruled out the possibility, or necessity, of conceiving political or economic arrangements of any complexity at all, after the overthrow of
capital. The conviction of an inherent simplification of administration
and production, economy and polity alike, found its most passionate
expression in the pages of *State and Revolution*, where any cook could
run the state. The legacy of institutional thought within classical
Marxism was thus always very weak, with dire consequences for the
actual process of institutionalization in Bolshevik Russia itself. The
post-classical tradition of Western Marxism did nothing to remedy
these deficiencies. It did, however, develop a range of philosophical
discourses projecting diverse transvaluations of an ideal-civilizational
character. The Frankfurt School, and thinkers more loosely associated
with it, was most fecund in these: Marcuse and Bloch, in particular,
produced overt varieties of moral-aesthetic utopia, Adorno oblique
elements of one. All these were pitched on a speculative plane entirely
remote from any existent social movement or political reality. Nevertheless, there can be no doubt of the positive heritage of this strand
within Western Marxism. It seems likely that, possibly by way of its
attenuated 'pedagogical' mutant in Habermas's theory of communication, this will prove a significant stimulus to creative attempts at
further transvaluations in the future.

13. See *Workers' Control and Socialist Democracy*, London 1982, pp 261-288; 'Power
and Production in a Classless Society', *Socialist Review*, No 59, September-October
1981, pp 36-82.

Nevertheless, it remains true that little or none of this work has touched on the actualization of a tangible socialist future. The institutional terrain has been characteristically neglected throughout. Yet it is quite clear that without serious exploration and mapping of it, any political advance beyond a parliamentary capitalism will continue to be blocked. No working-class or popular bloc in a Western society will ever make a leap in the dark, at this point in history, let alone into the grey on grey of an Eastern society of the type that exists today. A socialism that remains incognito will never be embraced by it.

To bring the two closer together, there are four great areas where practical research and proposal are above all now needed. (i) The first of these is this the political structure of a socialist democracy. What would be the precise forms of mandate, periodicity, franchise and constituency in a 'neo-soviet' system articulating workplace and residential principles within a producers' democracy covering polity and economy alike? How far would a professional administrative apparatus subsist? What division of powers would be codified? How would jurisdiction be allocated between national and local instances of authority? Would there exist a new 'technology of delegation'? What would be the optimal ways of disaggregating control over the means of communication? (ii) The second central area for debate is obviously the pattern of an advanced socialist economy. Assuming a full producers' democracy and popular determination of alternative plans, all the most difficult and intricate problems remain. What would be the range of forms of social ownership? How large, or small, a role should the market play? Could planning ever pre-adjust to new needs, with their inherent dynamism? What devices would exist to resolve conflicts between central and regional interests? What would be the appropriate combination of price mechanisms? How should consumer rights be articulated with those of producers, in major services? Should the volume of product choices be increased, or diminished? Which patterns of technology, and what distribution of labour-times, would be desirable? How should different jobs be remunerated? (iii) A third area where careful reflection is long overdue is what might be called the socio-cultural pattern of a 'libertarian levelling' — that is, means for abolishing class and gender inequalities beyond the reappropriation of the means of production by the direct producers. What kinds of detailed transformation of the educational system, and mutations of the division of labour, would most effectively tend to overcome any inherited or imposed ladder of life-chances — while at the same time multiplying rather than restricting individual differentiation and development of talent? (iv) The final and most formidable area of all concerns the international relations between — inevitably — unevenly developed socialist countries themselves. Ultimately, this involves the problem of the relationship between the producing classes in the rich nations and those of the poor nations, as well as the question of the relationship between the world peasantry and the world working-class within the poorer countries themselves. What would be any projectable pattern of equitable flows of trade and investment between North and South, were both liberated from the sway of capital? How could revenues and resources be progressively best shared? What kinds of technological exchange and diffusion would most depolarize the economic geography left by capitalism? Is 'evened development' historically imaginable — if so, what would it mean?

Merely to enumerate such questions is to register how little most of them have been directly confronted within the Marxist tradition in the West. It is against this background that the recent appearance of Alec Nove's *Economics of Feasible Socialism* is so significant a development. [14] In a work of luminous freshness and clarity, common sense and good humour, analytic logic and empirical detail, Nove has put to rest a century of unexamined preconceptions and illusions about what might lie on the other side of capital, and awakened us to our first real vision of what a socialist economy, under democratic control, might look like. The premises of that vision are a deft and elegant critique of the notion that labour-values could be pre-eminent in any form of rational calculation under socialism; that the market could ever be entirely substituted by the plan; that central planning itself could ever be free from antinomies of level in its hierarchy of decision-making; or that the division of labour could ever give way to pure permutation of skills and roles. Against all these misconceptions, Nove shows how central the criteria of scarcity and utility must be for the computation of values under socialism; how necessary the market and money remain, as the most efficient mediators of democratic microeconomic

14. London 1983.

choice, over a wide range of consumption; how far their preservation is from contradicting the overall guidance of a central plan, properly constructed and controlled; and how essential variegation of types of social property and enterprise will be, in any 'free association of producers'. His own preferred solutions envisage at least five major forms — from state ownership of basic producer goods industries and financial institutions, to self-managed socialized enterprises operating on a local scale, to cooperatives controlling their own property, small private ventures with a strict capital ceiling, and finally a great deal of skilled self-employment. The seduction of this model lies in its combination of realism and radicalism — a hallmark of much of the book as a whole. Far from the over-centralized plans and bureaucratic monopolies of the Communist states, with their vain attempts to suppress market and rig price relationships by administrative fiat, at great cost to producers and consumers alike, Nove's 'feasible socialism' is equally far from any of the Social-Democratic stand-ins for capitalism: all private ownership of the principal means of producion is abolished, in an economy where income differentials are held within a range of 1:2 or 1:3, a much more drastic compression than in even the most egalitarian of existing societies in the East.

Nove's book contains a polemic, memorable for its wit and absence of rancour, with the bulk of conventional Marxist wisdom on the subjects he discusses (though not with all Marxists, among whom Trotsky — as he points out — anticipated some of his conclusions). *The Economics of Feasible Socialism* is, in fact, perhaps the first central work of the post-war epoch about and for socialism that is clearly written from outside the Marxist tradition. As such, it represents a moral, as well as an intellectual, lesson to any Left that defines itself as Marxist: now put on notice to meet the same standards of honesty and acuity in its own contributions to ongoing discussions of any future socialism. This is not to say that Nove's work is beyond criticism. He rightly reproaches the main Marxist tradition for the utopianism of much of its conception of a socialist society — insisting, in terms virtually identical to those of Williams, that it is not simplicity but complexity that will characterize any realistic model of it. Yet his treatment of Marxism is also in a way a curiously forgetful one. For what confers its great authority on the book is its intimate knowledge, and close account, of the Soviet-style planned economies — reformed or unreformed, from their beginnings in the 20's down to the present. It is to these that Nove has devoted most of his scholarly life. A large part of the message of the book is precisely that no socialist democracy in the West could afford to ignore the detailed record of centralized planning in the East, simply on the self-satisfied grounds that it was bureaucratic, and therefore nothing to do with socialism. In that sense, the historical precondition of the theoretical achievement of *The Economics of Feasible Socialism* has been the cumulative practical experience of the attempts to construct socialism, in very hard and disadvantageous conditions, in the name of Marxism. No other historical experience is available to us: social-democracy yields few lessons for Nove's enterprise, and is essentially absent from his book. Behind it stands, not the vacuities of a Crosland — whose *Future of Socialism* is appropriately not so much as mentioned — but the insight and knowledge of reflections like Kornai's *Dilemmas of a Socialist Economy*.[15] The laboratory out of which Nove's realism has been forged is Eastern Europe and the Soviet Union.

That background also indicates, however, what is essentially missing from his work. How are we to get from where we are today to where he points us to tomorrow? There is no answer to this question in Nove. His halting discussion of 'transition' tails away into apprehensive admonitions to moderation to the British Labour Party, and pleas for proper compensation to capitalist owners of major industries, if these are to be nationalized. Nowhere is there any sense of what a titanic political change would have to occur, with what fierceness of social struggle, for the economic model of socialism he advocates ever to materialize. Between the radicalism of the future end-state he envisages, and the conservatism of the present measures he is prepared

15. For the cumulative work of Janos Kornai, see successively *Anti-Equilibrium*, Amsterdam 1971; *Economics of Shortage*, Amsterdam 1980; and *Growth, Shortage and Efficiency*, Oxford 1982 — a trio designed, as he explains in the latter (p 2), to set out general methodological foundations for the study of alternative economic systems; to contribute towards the microeconomic theory of a socialist economy; and finally to sketch a dynamic macroeconomic theory of such an economy. Practical observations on the Hungarian experience can be found in his above-cited lecture, *Dilemmas of a Socialist Economy*, Dublin 1979.

to countenance, there is an unbridgeable abyss. How could private ownership of the means of production ever be abolished by policies less disrespectful of capital than those of an Allende or a Benn, which he reproves? What has disappeared from the pages of *The Economics of Feasible Socialism* is virtually all attention to the historical dynamics of any serious conflict over the control of the means of production, as the record of the 20th century demonstrates them. If capital could visit such destruction on even so poor and small an outlying province of its empire as Vietnam, to prevent its loss, is it likely that it would suffer its extinction meekly in its own homelands? The lessons of the past sixty-five years or so are in this respect without ambiguity or exception: there is no case, from Russia to China, from Vietnam to Cuba, from Chile to Nicaragua, where the existence of capitalism has been challenged, and the furies of intervention, blockade and civil strife have not descended in response. Any viable transition to socialism in the West must seek to curtail that pattern: but to shrink from or to ignore it is to depart from the world of the possible altogether. In the same way, to construct an economic model of socialism in one advanced country is a legitimate exercise: but to extract it from any computable relationship with a surrounding, and necessarily opposing, capitalist environment — as this work does — is to locate it in thin air. The irony of Nove's enterprise is that a work which sets out to be resolutely realistic at every point should be based on a typically utopian abstraction of actual historical reality, and its empirical field of forces. In putting that history out of mind, *The Economics of Feasible Socialism* falls subject to the very criticism it so often makes of Marxism: it proceeds on the basis of manifestly unrealistic assumptions about how people behave — once they are organized in antagonistic classes. In that sense, only a *Politics of Feasible Socialism* could rescue it from the realm of utopian thought it seeks to escape.

No single book, however, could hope to encompass the totality of problems posed by a transition to socialism beyond bureaucracy as well as capital. There is something of the civil servant he once was, in the best sense, in Nove's approach to that socialism: an expert brief, explaining lucidly and precisely, with a certain detachment, what practical arrangements would be suitable if an option were to be made for such a society. In some ways, this very distance from the heat and battle of politics is what gives his work its peculiar force of attraction. Freed from any strategic calculation, informed only by the patent generosity and decency that incline the author — *ceteris paribus* — towards a juster economic order, the resultant image of a possible society is so sensible and winning that it is likely to do more to create converts to socialism than any other recent work, from a more conventional or committed background on the Left.

There are a number of conclusions to be drawn. A shift from the axis of values to that of institutions, in projections of a socialist or communist future, has been much needed, and must bring with it a new sense of practical complexities. But that shift does not in itself represent a move out of the utopian space as such, so long as it is dissociated from any plausible analysis of the historical processes capable of realizing values or institutions alike. This is not to depreciate either emphasis. On the contrary, the example we have just looked at demonstrates how important a contribution can be made by a sustained effort to think through the problems of a possible socialism from within that space. Further explorations of it, in fact, would benefit from a more active dialectic between the reshaping of values and re-designing of institutions, in which each worked as a mediation or control of the other, to permit new kinds of opening. It is noteworthy that the two major impulses towards bridging the gulf between 'institutional' and 'ideal' discourses of change have in recent years lain largely outside the ambit of socialist discussion proper. These have come from the women's movement and the ecological movement. Each has raised issues which are at once of the most far-reaching and fundamental sort conceivable — relations between the sexes, relations between humanity and nature, which lie athwart rather than within the relations between classes that is the central concern of Marxism — yet which at the same time have permitted ready articulation into short-range practical objectives. The margin of error or even mystification that has on occasion accreted around each is inevitable enough. But what is impressive is the *ease of transition* within them across the whole gamut from the most metaphysical transvaluations of existing relations to the most mundane institutional amendments of them. It is probably not fortuitous that the one body of current work on the contours of an alternative socialism that does occupy a creative middle register between these two, combining philosophical reflection and practical proposal in a distinctive synthesis, should be the very original work of André Gorz, nourished directly by ecological concerns.[16]

To conclude, then. Not every prospect of human emancipation coincides with the advent of socialism, which has no monopoly on utopian discourse today. Not every contribution to socialism as a body of thought coincides with the output of Marxism, which has no monopoly of critical theory on the Left either. Where does this leave historical materialism, in the 80's? In a sense, where it has always been: at the cross-roads of past and future, economics and politics, history and strategy — that is, at the centre of all socialist reference today, even where it would surpass it. Such centrality is not exclusivity. Claims for the latter were always unfounded. The bases of the former, however, persist for reasons that the counter-examples I have cited themselves suggest. For historical materialism remains the only intellectual paradigm capacious enough to to be able to link the ideal horizon of a socialism to come with the practical contradictions and movements of the present, and their descent from structures of the past, in a theory of the distinctive dynamics of social development as a whole. Like any long-term programme of research in the traditional sciences themselves, it has known periods of repetition or arrest, generated in its time errors and misdirections. But like any other such paradigm, it will not be replaced so long as there is no superior candidate for comparable overall advance in knowledge. There is no sign of that yet, and we can therefore be confident that at least as much work will be done within Marxism tomorrow as it is today. The working class in the West is currently in disarray, in the throes of one of those far-reaching recompositions that have periodically marked its history since the Industrial Revolution; but it is much less defeated and dispersed than it was during the last Great Depression, and — short of war — has many days still ahead of it. Marxism has no reason to abandon its Archimedean vantage-point: the search for subjective

16. See especially the remarkable second half of *Adieux au Proletariat*, Paris 1980, and *Les Chemin du Paradis*, Paris 1983. These make an interesting comparison with Nove's work. The problem of political vectors in the present, for the cultural values or economic practices of the future, obtains here too.

agencies capable of effective strategies for the dislodgement of objective structures. But amidst pervasive changes within world capitalism today, those three terms can only be successfully combined if they have a common end that is at once desirable and believable for millions who are now hesitant or indifferent to them. That condition is still a long way off, by any calculation. But we can be sure that it will not be reached without a flow of the mainstream tradition of socialism, the current of historical materialism, towards it.

Index